WIVES WHO WIN

How to Win in Your Marriage God's Way

Monique Thank
you so for your support
appreciate you

Treal Ravenel

Also by Treal Ravenel

A Winning Wife is a Praying Wife "90 Day Devotional on Winning Daily in your Marriage."

The Transformation Process According to Proverbs "For the Next 31 Days."

Rolling with the Punches "Learning to Triumph in the Midst of Adversity."

Speak Life "31 Powerful Affirmations that will Change your Life."

The Wilderness Journey "Keys to Unlock Your Spiritual Freedom"

Dedication

To my oldest nieces: Te'Aire, Taije, and god-daughter Zaniyah:

I know that each of you desire to one day meet the perfect guy and experience the joys and happiness of marriage. It is my prayer that even in your single season of life that you will never stop working on becoming the most authentic version of yourself. I pray that as you create a life that you are pleased with, that self-development and growth will always be at the top of your list. As I often tell each of you; the better you are, the better your relationships and, one-day, marriage will be. I am excited about what is to come for each of you and believe that you will be a *Wife Who Wins* in the appropriate timing and season of your life.

Love you dearly,
Auntie/god-mother

Acknowledgement

I would like to thank my husband, Henry L. Ravenel Jr., for giving me the space and time to steal away to complete this book. I started writing this book in 2016, and typically it doesn't take long for me to write, however, I ran into so many mental blocks a.k.a. writer's block. For the life of me, I could not finish it. I got to a certain point and got stuck. I prayed and asked God what the deal with that was and he gave me instructions to go on a two-day sabbatical away from home in order to complete the book. I spoke to my husband about it, and he was 100% supportive of my decision. Not only did I complete the book but I was able to finish some other projects for the Wives Who Win community, which will launch soon.

I am so thankful to have a loving, understanding, and loyal husband; not just to me, but to my purpose and ministry. He often encourages me, lifts me in prayer and praises in reminding me that I and what I have been called to do is necessary. He has brought out the best in me. This book would not be a success without him. I often tease and say that my husband does not have a filter, and sometimes I appreciate the direct approach. It keeps me all the way together.

I would like to thank every wife that is in the Wives Who Win and Detour Movement Inc. community for keeping me accountable to my purpose and God's vision in holding the space for wives.

Thanks to all those who contributed to this book. I solicited testimonials from wives who are winning in their marriage, and they were so kind and excited to share. To

Ne'shama Bonneau, Felicia Stevenson, Karen Guikoume, Shauntay Dunning, Curtisha Grant and Naomi Burrell thank you, ladies, for sharing your stories. It is my hope that your stories will encourage other wives to win in their marriage.

Thanks to Lenia's Graphixx for the winning book cover and our editor Cleveland McLeish for practically being on standby whenever we need him to edit a book, or other content.

Table of Contents

Introduction

I know all too well of what adversity looks like. The enemy has had his fair share of putting his hand to the plow in my life and marriage. Challenges and opposition will come, and it does put pressure on the marriage, however, it doesn't have to destroy your marriage. As a wife, you have the upper hand. As a wife, you set the tone and temperature of your home. It is your scent that will drive all possibilities of hope.

I learned early on how my attitude in my marriage and toward my husband would be a game changer. I stopped focusing on little things that didn't matter and started focusing on things that would yield positive results in my marriage.

I grabbed hold of my power and made a decision that I was a Wife Who Wins. Against all the odds, impossibilities, craziness or chaos; I am a Wife Who Wins.

My choice to Win not only benefits me, but those around me. God told me in 2016 that He wanted me to remind wives all over the world that they are Winners.

I have had the opportunity to sit in the company of dozens of wives from different walks of life, from many different parts of the world. Some that I have spoken to expressed to me how discontent, unhappy or dissatisfied they are in their marriage. Sometimes it's because of marital differences or adversity that has caused great distance, lack of communication or even, in some cases, separation. Some are just simply going along to get along because of children, joint property or whatever the case may be. Other reasons are due to personal discontentment or the lack of growth and maturity on one or both sides, and the other person is simply tired. A vast majority are unhappy or discontent because they are waiting for their husbands to change and create happiness and satisfaction in their lives.

I wanted to make some noise in the marriage community in letting wives know they have what it takes to WIN in their marriage. You don't have to go day to day unhappy and sorrowful, even if you have experienced some crazy things or times in your marriage. You can decide today that this is the first day of the rest of your life, and from this day forward; you will be a 100% contributor to Winning in your Marriage God's Way.

Some may ask, well doesn't my husband have to be onboard as well? The answer is yes, and I will go out on a limb and say most men want to win in their marriage as well. Hence, *why* they made a lifetime commitment to get married. The fact that he isn't as in tuned as you are, doesn't mean he isn't on board or that he will not get onboard. It could mean that he is trying to figure it out as much as you are, but in his own way and in his own time, which is unpredictable by the way. Men are different, the way they process and decode information and circumstances are different. The way they handle things even if they seem important or a priority to us is different. While women want to get to the bottom of it and won't quit until we do so, men sometimes ignore it, focus on something else or create a divergent all together, so they won't have to face or deal with the real issue right then and there. They tend to do things on their own time and rather not feel pressured, coerced, or manipulated. A man handling it and women handling it is entirely different, and you have to accept that truth.

Because you decided to purchase this book suggest that you are committed to handling it, and because you are; God honors that. Your decision to better your marriage starts with you, and your marriage will benefit as a result. You have a strong influence in the marriage covenant, and this book can very well be the breakthrough you needed all along.

How do I stay Grounded:
① Spending time w/ God
② Reading His word

What do I lack for self-growth
① Security
② Communication
③ Boldness
④ Jealousy

Part I

* Never thought I was good
enough to be loved b/c of
my weight
* Never felt I had a voice to
share my feelings
* I have been afraid of rejection
people not liking me
* Always being substituted for
what seemed someone better!
→ In order to be successful in defeating
the disapperoval of others embody true
unquestionalbee evidence of who you
are.

Chapter 1
Back to the Basics- the Foundation

Throughout the course of my life, whenever I wanted an academic or career promotion, I had to prepare myself accordingly. In school, I had to study for the exam to make an acceptable grade to go onto the next level. Likewise, during my career, I had to ensure I was competent before I received a raise or promotion of any kind. In school, I had to study long and hard, often making sacrifices in other areas. I planned and prepared because I wanted the best grade.

I did the same for the jobs I wanted, although I wasn't aiming for a better grade, but more pay. Why is it that many people do not prepare the same way for marriage? Why is it that so many don't take the same time, effort and investment to ensure that they are prepared mentally, socially, emotionally and spiritually for marriage? The investment I am referring to is the one each woman need to make for themselves, and that is self-development and growth. Many women think because they have accomplished life success, matured in numerical age and maybe doing well in other areas; that they have mastered self. That couldn't be further from the truth. In my case, in particular, there were a lot of things that I accomplished, including successfully single-handedly raising my son, who is now in College. I have a winning career, possess two degrees, graduated undergraduate with honors (Cum Lade) and graduate school with a 3.8 GPA. I am a property owner, business owner, investor, spiritually grounded and the list goes on. I don't say this to boast, but I am making a point that there were still some areas of my life that had not yet evolved, despite all of my accomplishments, and it was evident in the very beginning of my marriage.

I did what a lot of you are still doing. I focused heavily on my career, education and spiritual growth; but did not pay too much attention to my self-development and growth needs (internal growth). Honestly, I felt the more accomplished I was in other areas; it would automatically take care of the internal growth when it came to my social, mental and emotional well-being. I thought because my spiritual relationship was so developed, that I would be the perfect wife and develop a perfect life from day one of my marriage. I would hear others talk about how marriage was work and how you have to work daily to make it work, but I didn't think that applied to me, because I had God on my side. I was silly to rely only on my spiritual capabilities for a relationship that involved both a spiritual and natural outlook and investment.

My failure to do the necessary self-growth work did affect my marriage in the beginning. There were arguments and adversity that could have been avoided or handled a lot differently had I taken the time to invest in the most important person in my life, ME! Yes, YOU! You are the most important person in your life, God being first, and you are worth the investment. Your husband and children are worth the investment. I often say your marriage will be as good as you. That goes for every other relationship in your life. When you take the time out to do the self-growth work, it is reflective in other areas and relationships in your life. Even if you desire to start a ministry or business or currently have one; those relationships will be reflective of your self-growth and development, or the lack thereof. Those relationships are also a reflection of the existing relationships that you have, in particular, your marriage.

While so many focus on the big day (the Wedding) and doing life together; the ultimate focus should be on planning, preparing and positioning yourself before the big day so that you do life successfully together. Even if you, like me, didn't *heavily* focus on your self-growth and development before marriage; I can assure that it is not too late. You can start today looking at areas in your life that need improving and make a decision to work on these areas. If it is a bad attitude, selfish behavior, unruly tongue, bad moods / attitudes, bitterness, low self-esteem, lack of self-love and acceptance, un-forgiveness, past hurt/pain, spirit of control or manipulation, rebelliousness, envy, jealousy, anger, bitterness, ~~unforgiveness~~ or others; you can choose today to be better. If you are struggling with any of those areas mentioned, I know it is affecting your marriage and you cannot tell me otherwise. Because of those areas, you and your husband have had barriers built that have caused either lack of communication, lack of love demonstrated, lack of sex and intimacy, lack of respect, lack of trust, lack of honesty and lack in many other areas. If this is where you stand today, I am here to tell you that there is still hope! You can make a decision today that these things will no longer prevent you from being a Wife Who Wins and they will cease to have a say in your marriage.

There are some things you can do to help with the self-growth and development process, but the very first thing is Identification. You have to first identify which of these areas are affecting you, your marriage and other relationships. Once you have identified those things; find out the root cause of it. Why does it exist? Where does it stem from? Who or what caused it? Keep in mind, when trying to determine who or what, because this does not have to be an outside person or factor; it could very well be you. Then ask yourself a very profound question and answer it: Why have I given this thing or person so much power over my life? After you do this, then you want to begin the process of removing and releasing it from your life to never return again. That in itself is a process and can take some time - please do not expect an overnight victory. To be more in control of your emotions and feelings; you have to first understand why they exist so you can determine how to manage them. Let me just say this, it is okay to acknowledge how you feel and even express it, but it is never okay to allow how you feel to have complete control over you or the decisions you make.

Getting Back to the Basics — the Foundation is simply getting back or in touch with who you are. It is being able to understand you as a person, not as a wife, mother, leader, business owner, etc., but you as an individual, a woman. Identify your inner self and the different behaviors or moods that have taken away from who you are; your true authentic self. I heard Pastor Rick Warren say that you can't truly be authentic until you admit how unauthentic you really are. Allow yourself to go through the necessary healing or deliverance process that you may have robbed yourself of, for whatever the reason. The foundation of you is the version of yourself that God created and desires for you to live up to. When you identify and reveal that person, you will not only reap the rewards in your marriage, but in every area of your life.

Getting Back to the Basics Reflection:

How many times have you asked yourself the question, "Who am I and Why was I born?" I know I asked myself this before and it is okay if you did as well. This question came at a time when I didn't have a relationship with God — when I was trying to figure out and do life my way. I was all sorts of confused and detached from my true sense of self. When I stumbled across two scriptures in the Bible; I was relieved that someone else already figured it out for me. No longer did I have to try and do life my way and attempt to create my own results. These very two scriptures are what I will give you to read and meditate on. Don't do it just because I said so - do it because you know deep within that you need to identify who that person is that God created. Do it because you need this person to come alive so you can be a better woman, a better wife, a better mother, employee, employer or leader. Do it because your marriage depends on it.

Once you read, meditate and have a full understanding of these two scriptures; email us at officialwiveswhowin@gmail.com and tell us what you got out of these two scriptures and how you plan to apply them to your life and marriage going forward.

Scriptures:

Jeremiah 1:5
Jeremiah 29:11

NEXT, take a step further and connect with our Wives Who Win Club via Facebook @ https://www.facebook.com/groups/273276863146874/

*The ones that left was never my choice for you. Ebonee and those other kids were just that, kids and kids will do what kids do. You are grown now and are no longer a child so stop carrying around childish <u>wounds</u>

① To over come rejection be your authentic self.

* for the next 7 nights don't turn your back on your husband out of expectation of ~~you~~ what you desire from him but give him yourself. Which is tender hearted, soft and full of compassion. Do this not expecting him to reciprocate. "You" will melt his hard exterior!

Chapter 2
Complete Surrender is a Necessity

According to Miriam-Webster online dictionary, surrender means to "to yield to the power, control, or possession of another upon compulsion or demand." Complete surrender is to give of absolute power or control to something or someone else preferably who is stronger than you, and that has your best interest at heart. That person in which I speak of is God, the Father. I am not only referring to you surrendering but at some point, you will need to surrender your marriage to God as well. The reason that is important is because you will not continue to do life your way in yielding your results which have not been all that favorable anyway.

Surrendering is giving up your will and allowing God's will to drive your life and decisions. I can tell you that God's will for your life are perfect and it will always benefit you, whether you believe that or not. Because I struggled with being in control for a long time, I didn't think that God's will was the best for me. I gave God pieces of me,; those I thought He could handle and those I felt I could handle,; I kept for myself. What I failed to realize at that time was that surrendering would help characterize or influence my entire life by desiring to maintain unbroken fellowship and oneness with God. Surrendering would help me to model after the character of Jesus.

While I thought God was trying to control me as if I was some puppet or taking something away from me; he was trying to get something to me. By me surrendering my life and relationships to God, I totally handed it over. I relinquished full control and told God he was the most important and necessary part of my life. I confessed aloud and silently that I could live without anyone and anything else, but I couldn't live without Him.

Some of you may be reading this and saying I sound like a complete fool. To you, I may, but what I can tell you is that when I decided to surrender completely, blessings overtook my life and marriage like crazy and still are until this day. And speaking of a fool; the Bible says in Proverbs 1: 7 that the fear *(regard, reverence, highly esteem which come with surrendering)* of the LORD is the beginning of knowledge, but fools despise wisdom and instruction.

You see, surrendering helped me to put things in its proper perspective as it related to my role as a woman - a wife, mother, and leader. I used to have a terrible attitude and when I didn't get my way, oh it was apparent alright, and that behavior showed up righteously in my relationships and marriage, including my relationship with God. When I didn't get my way, I was disobedient, self-indulged, selfish and deceitful. When you feel like your life is your own, you operate in all kinds of ugly. Many of you may recall the story of Jonah in the Bible. He was the guy who got swallowed by the big fish and stayed in the fish belly for three days and three nights. Let me break it down for you in my language. God gave Jonah instructions to go to Ninevah to preach and warn the city of a pending destruction, but Jonah *(out of fear and disobedience — refusal to surrender)* felt like he would go the opposite way and do the opposite of what God told him. This sounds to me like somebody wanted to be in control of their own life and destiny. So Jonah did that, he caught a ferry (boat), paid his fees and got on. He went to the bottom of the ship and fell asleep.

God caused a great storm, and the boat started rocking ~~like~~ uncontrollably and threatened to go to the bottom of the sea. The sailors started getting scared and were trying to figure out what in the world happened that quickly to cause a storm that *was now*~~is~~ threatening their lives. After a few discussions amongst ~~themselves~~*themselves* and then one with Jonah after waking him from his deep sleep; it was *apparent*~~determined~~ that Jonah was the cause of the storm and he had to go. So eventually the sailors picked Jonah up and threw him overboard~~,~~ and a big fish *caught and* swallowed him. While in the fish; Jonah cried out to God and was pitiful. I believe he was sorry for being disobedient and didn't realize how his disobedience — failure to surrender to God's will — would cost his life or threaten the lives of others. Needless to say, the big fish regurgitated Jonah, and he landed on the beach after*ward;* he made a decision to surrender to God. *He eventually went*~~He then went to~~ Ninevah to preach, warned the people, and they were saved.

How many of you reading this right now have been like Jonah sometime in your life? *How many of you are Jonah now?* You felt that obeying or surrendering to God would not get you the results you desired, so you chose or are still choosing your own way. In doing so, you got *are* trapped or caught up in something or a scandal and are crying out to God to save you. For these purposes; your failure to surrender has affected your life significantly and now that you are married; it is affecting your marriage as well. You tried doing marriage your way. You looked at the celebrity marriages on reality TV and tried implementing some of their ways, but it didn't work. You looked at marriages on social media and those around you and tried to do some of the same things that they are doing, and that didn't *didn't* work for your marriage either. Listen, it is Your Marriage, so that means it is Your Process. The only anecdote for you and this cause is to surrender yourself to God completely. For me, one of the areas was my attitude, but for you, it may be something else.

It is not about what you feel is best or what will make you feel better at the time. You have to stay attentive to the voice of God and walk according to his ways, and you can only do that by surrendering. To be a wife who wins, you have to be able to hear from God clearly; have a level of discernment *(ability to judge well)* and have the spirit of Christ living on the inside of you. The fruit of His Spirit must be evident in your life daily, and they will show up by your ability to love; to be kind, gentle, and peaceful, maintain self-control, be faithful, joyful, and gentle.

Surrendering is more about others, than it is about you. Just look at the story of Jonah; he almost destroyed an entire city (Ninevah) and the sailors on the boat because he refused to surrender. Don't be like Jonah and allow your failure to yield destroy you or your marriage. When you surrender, you increase the chances of others surrendering to God as well; that includes your husband and children.

Complete Surrender Reflection:

If you know that your inability or unwillingness to be a Wife Who Win has a direct correlation with your decision to completely surrender to God; I want to invite you to make a decision today to do so. Making this decision can, and will, remove the limitations from your marriage. As you submit to God, you can willingly and unselfishly submit to your husband. You will value the meaning of true love and respect and will offer it, not because your husband deserves it, but because of your love and respect for God. What will you choose?

If you desire additional support, it is available to you. Email us at officialwiveswin@gmail.ceom for your complimentary 30-minute consultation. Be sure you are connected to our Facebook page by going to **facebook.com/wiveswhowin**.

I need you to take one step futher in surrendering and connect with our Wives Who Win Club via Facebook @ https://www.facebook.com/groups/273276863146874/..
This group will offer you the level of support and accountablity you need on your journey to surrender.

Chapter 3
Deal with your U.G.L.Y.

As I mentioned in Chapter 1, for a long time I focused heavily on my spiritual growth. I pursued the lifestyle in learning how to pray, fast, and read*ing* the *Bible* ~~Word~~ regularly, but I did not ask God to reveal my ugly to me. I was so focused on the spiritual aspect of my walk and not necessarily concerned about other areas in my life. In a sense, I thought I was the perfect Christian because of my solid relationship with God. There were things about me that I felt I conquered, but the truth was because there were no daily triggers, my issues were still there but perfectly masked. I was still dealing with some internal ugliness and denying that did not change the fact that it was still true. Little did I know that my inner ugliness would affect my marriage in the way it did early on.

Going to church and being involved in ministry is what you should do as a follower of Christ, however; those things alone will not produce change within, especially when dealing with your internal ugliness. Two critical relationships are essential before you can have a healthy and successful marriage. Number one; your relationship with God has to be Rock Solid. Number two: your relationship with yourself has to be Rock Solid. You must be in a position where you are asking God to show you your internal ugliness daily.

If your marriage is on the rocks and has been in an awkward place for some time now, you need to ask God why. I know many of you were taught not to question God, but I want to dispel that lie today and give you permission to ask God why. In asking God why, you are not questioning His authority or posittion, but you are asking him to reveal to you what or how you have contributed to the awkwardness or weirdness in your marriage. Let's face it, we all face levels of weirdness, and it is okay but we want to get from a place of weirdness to a place of reveal. In the reveal place, you are asking God to explain to you what it is about you that is prolonging this unwanted state in your marriage and preventing the happiness and joy that you desire to experience.

When my husband and I were going through our awkwardness, I pointed the finger at him. I wanted to list all the reasons why he was the issue for that awkward place. I totally dismissed and denied any contribution. There were patterns, not only in my marriage but in previous relationships that went sour that I completely ignored. I had to step outside of the frame and view the picture from the same view others saw it from and make a decision to deal with the deepest and darkest parts of my inner core.

The inner core of anything is not visible to the human or natural eye. Think about the core of the earth. *"The earth's core comprises a solid inner core and liquid outer core; both made mostly of iron. Outside of these parts is the mantle, then the crust on which we live. Earth scientists have theorized that the Earth's core is responsible for the planet's magnetic field as well as plate tectonics."* (Woodhouse, 2017) There are some issues within your inner core (internally) that will be extremely hard to detect just at a glance or if everything appears to be okay. One would have to do some deep digging or soul searching to peel back the mantle (layers), breaking the iron and removing the liquid to see the unrevealed internal issues.

Have you seen the movie 'The Day After Tomorrow?' It was a science fiction film where a climatologist, Jack Hall (Dennis Quaid), was largely ignored by U.N. officials when presenting his environmental concerns; his research proves true when an enormous "superstorm" develops, setting off catastrophic natural disasters throughout the world. Trying to get to his son, Sam (Jake Gyllenhaal), who was trapped in New York with his friend Laura (Emmy Rossum) and others, Jack and his crew had to travel by foot from Philadelphia, braving the elements, to get to Sam before it was too late.

In the same way Jack attempted to warn the U.N. before things got ugly; I am trying to warn you before your internal ugly sets off catastrophic disasters throughout your marriage. I don't believe any issue or problem in marriage is irreparable, but I do believe the longer you ignore an issue or problem, the worst it becomes and the harder it is to repair. What if the U.N. listened to Jack initially and did something about the issue before it actually became an issue? It is like ignoring the elephant in the room and still trying to function normally; it would be super weird.

If ugly things are going on in your marriage, then it is time to get to the root and shift your focus and prayer life. If you are like me and prayed to God only to change your husband, I want you to now shift and ask God to change you. Ask God to show you the deep things only you and Him know about that is causing, contributing or even prolonging the unhappy state in your marriage. It is God's desire for you to win in your marriage. Marriage is supposed to be enjoyable and fulfilling, not daunting and draining. This is about YOU, not your husband, but you have to be willing and ready to take things to another level in understanding that you play a significant role in the success of your marriage. Your marriage sinking or succeeding has just as much to do with you as it does your husband.

This process is not going to be easy, in fact, it can be outright ugly (no pun intended) because you may feel you are over certain attitudes, behaviors, moods, etc. For some of you, your husband may have confronted some of the issues, and instead of receiving it as constructive criticism (regardless of his delivery) you viewed it as criticism, and immediately you punched back with your defense boxing gloves. I know for me, my husband would point out certain things he saw as a pattern and instead of me receiving it and taking the time to see why he still saw certain things I thought for sure were no longer an issue; I went in verbally swinging. I immediately got on the defense train. It was immature and displayed a lack of mental and emotional growth and lack of respect toward my husband.

If someone, be it your spouse, friend, children, etc. are saying things about you, I encourage you to take heed. Especially if what they are saying are things that you once struggled with, caused issued in previous relationships, has been a roadblock or barrier for you progressing in the past or in other areas – this isn't the time to get offended, but the time to shut up, listen up and change up. Apparently, there is some residue or a stench that is showing up all around you and you sista girl can't run or hide any longer – deal with your Ugly before it deals with your marriage! Even if your feelings are hurt at the time, because the truth hurts – still listen. As you are listening, observe what they are saying to you about you and say, "Self, is there some truth to what they are saying?"

Some of my ugliness was: Control, Manipulation, Rebellious (nasty attitude) and a Mouth that would tear you all the way down. I am ashamed to say, but yep that was my truth. If you read my book: *Rolling with the Punches "Triumphing in the Midst of Adversity"*, I shared how being in an abusive and toxic relationship contributed to these ugly behaviors and how it caused other relationships to fail. When you are in an unequally yoked relationship; whatever internal demons (ugliness) that person is dealing with will eventually grab ahold of you. How? Every time you connect with that person sexually, a part of that person is released within you. Have you ever heard of soul ties? There are physical, mental, emotional, and spiritual aspects of sexual intercourse. There is so much emotional bondage that is associated with sexual immortality, and it shows up differently, for example: soul ties. That is why God is against pre-marital sex, not because He doesn't want us to enjoy life, but He understands what the cost of enjoying life can bring for you and your future relationships. Read 1 Corinthians 6:12-20 to learn more about that.

As I prepare to end this chapter, start thinking about **what** it is that is showing up in your marriage, **why** it is showing up in your marriage, **where/who** did it come from and **how** you are going to deal with it before it deals with your marriage in the worst way.

If you want to change bad enough, when God shows you your internal ugliness; you have to be willing and intentional about the change that is required and be ready to do the work. Your prayers at this point should be geared toward asking God to give you the strength to change; ask Him to help you see the inner parts of you that have caused the current craziness and to help you to be honest with yourself.

Because I am committed to you being a Wife Who Wins; I want to give you 10 Commandments to having a Great Marriage:

I.   Honor God with your first fruits and with the substance of all the increase. God gets and keeps the first part of you.

II.   Your body is God's temple, so treat it as such. Honor God with your body by the decisions you make every single day. This includes your daily upkeep.

III.   Continue contributing and growing your current relationships by applying these things written throughout these chapters. Your other relationships will only be as good as your marriage.

IV. Cleanliness is next to Godliness so practice such in your singleness so you can transfer it into your marriage. If you are already married, start practicing so that it becomes consistent. When I talk of cleanliness, I'm not talking only about externally but internal cleanliness; your thoughts, behaviors, and attitudes.

V. Get rid of selfishness. Willingly share what you have with your husband.

VI. We serve a God of compassion and as a kingdom ~~citizen~~*citizen;* we should implement that same attribute toward others. Show compassion toward your husband. (Ephesians 4:32; Matthew 6:14-15)

VII. Know, understand and practice the fruit of the Spirit (Galatians 5 22-23). Implement these into your life and relationships every single day. Be intentional about the fruit that shows up in your marriage.

VIII. Get rid of fault-finding and practice Grace and Forgiveness. Forgive, because God first forgave you. (Ephesians 4:32)

IX. Choose to love those in your life the way God loves you and read and meditate on 1 Corinthians 13: 1-10. Love your husband the way God loves him.

X. Stay true to yourself. Be honest with who you are and be okay & accept that there is always room to grow. It is never too late for you to work on your spiritual or personal growth. The better you are, the better your marriage will become *and all other relationships that follow.*⸱

Bonus: Healed people help heal others; get healed so your marriage can WIN!

Deal with Your U.G.L.Y. Reflection:

U: Ugly (deeply rooted issues that are contributing to the ugly in your marriage)
G: Go to God in prayer on behalf of YOU
L: Look at YOU through the lens of God
Y: You are responsible for doing the work

1. What are some things about you that are causing, contributing or even prolonging the unhappy state in your marriage?
2. What are some things that are within your power to do or say that you can immediately or soon implement to begin contributing to the health, wealth, and happiness of your marriage?
3. Are you committed to doing these things?
4. When and how do you plan to do it?

If your Ugly is on the verge of destroying your marriage and you need help, contact us @ officialwiveswho@gmail.com for a FREE 1-on-1 30-minute consultation. Put in the subject line: I Am Ready to Deal with My Ugly.

Chapter 4
The Power of an Effective and Strategic Prayer Life

For the past few years, I have had a pretty consistent prayer life. I pray daily, sometimes multiple times per day, and on some days I pray longer than others. I learned prayer strategies years ago via ~~my~~ a former Pastor, and one significant thing he taught me among others is the Power of Praying the word (scriptures).

There is a scripture in Isaiah 55: 11 that says "So is my word that goes from my mouth: It will not return unto me empty, but will accomplish what I desire and achieve the purpose for which I sent it."

Jeremiah 1:12 says "The LORD said to me, "You have seen correctly, for I am watching to see that my word is fulfilled"

Basically, when you pray the word (scriptures) correctly; God hears and answers those prayers, and they will not go unanswered. I can honestly say that knowing the word and worth of prayer is something that has been deeply rooted in my bloodline on both sides of my family. In my book "*Rolling with the Punches*"; I shared how my mom would pace the floors *in our home* all night and morning praying about any and everything because she understood the power *and significance of effective and strategic*~~of~~ prayer.

When I got married, it was natural for me to pray diligently and fervently for my marriage and husband. Not because everything was wrong. but because prayer is a very powerful weapon and you get results when used in the right content and context. You may be saying, 'Treal is it that serious?' Well, I assure you that it is. In the same way; other things like a firearm, for instance, is a very powerful weapon. If used incorrectly or irresponsibly, it can cause more harm than good. I am ashamed to say but I used to pray incorrectly for my husband and marriage. I was very sincere in my prayers but sincerely wrong. When there were things about my husband that bothered me, I would immediately pray that God would change him. I would pray diligently and fervently for God's holy and righteous hand to go upside his head. And get this; I would even fast along with my praying in hopes of getting the results I wanted. I would sashay my holy self around and was very self-righteous and prideful because I was so confident in my walk with the Lord.

I used the scriptures as one of my powerful weapons and would chastise my husband on a regular basis. I chastised him for not praying how or when I prayed; for not praying long or hard enough like me; for not being spiritual enough in my eyes; for not making certain decisions or handling things the way I would. I chastised and judged him for not living up to my standards. Do you see a trend here? When I tell you that I was truly a hot holy mess, believe me when I say it. I was a judgmental, over analytical, mouthy wife and that caused tension and distance between me and my husband. Little did I know;

that at the time, although my heart was in the right place, my words and prayers were in a left field somewhere.

Part of the problem was that before I got married, I mapped out specifically how *I wanted* my marriage ~~would~~ *to* be. In my mind, I planned the perfect wedding, the perfect reception, and ultimately the perfect life. But after the celebration, we both had an ounce of reality. In fact, we both had to face the reality of one another in learning to appreciate and unconditionally love the true authentic version of one another. We had to learn to accept one another's differences, instead of trying to change or fix every little thing we didn't like about each other. *My husband had to learn how to be a Ephesians 5:25-55 husband; and I ~~─~~had to learn to how to be a 1 Peter 3:1-8 wife. We both simply had to learn.* ─This was everything from my husband not helping with the dishes, to me leaving water all over the bathroom *counter and floor* when I was done using it *to other things*. All too often, couples get married and have a false sense of hope and expectation for their marriage relationship. That in itself leads to a place of unhappiness and discontentment within the marriage. When you are discontent, your prayers then are solely focused on self-gratification and satisfaction aka selfishness.

I believe that for you to experience true happiness and fulfillment within your marriage, you first have to experience this in your own life. Being happy and fulfilled has something to do with your husband but it doesn't at the same time. I learned that you cannot control another grown up but what you can do is show up as the truest version of yourself.

One day when I was praying for God to change my husband, I heard Him say, "No, you change." I replied, "What God, no way — not me. I am Mrs. Holy Ghost Roller and I speak with the tongues of angels —— my life is flawless, none to compare, so certainly I heard you wrong." God assured me that He was talking to me and before I can could pray for my husband to change, the change would first need to start and be exemplified in my life. That crushed me because I swore that I was untouchable. It wasn't long after that I had to accept the fact that I had some things that God needed to do within me. My prayers went from, *'God change my husband' to 'God show me ——ME. Teach me by way of your Holy Spirit to be the wife you have called me to be. Remove from me everything not like you, including my self-righteous and prideful attitude. Lord show me through Your Word how I am supposed to conduct myself as a wife but not just a wife, but a holy and righteous wife.'* I wasn't trying to be deep but truly needed God to do something amazing in me so he could do something amazing in my marriage. To be holy is to live a dedicated and consecrated life to God (to be set apart) and to be righteous; to conduct oneself in a good way — virtuous, excellent and to live according to morals and standards. I wanted my life to exemplify Christ, and in doing that, my marriage would follow suit.

God put me together, and my prayers for my husband changed as well. They became pure and focused on God building him as the man he purposed for him to be as a husband, father, entrepreneur, ministry leader, and community influencer. I asked God to show me areas of his life I needed to pray for and in what fashion and God told me to pray "Thy Kingdom come and Thy Will be done" in my husband's life. When I shifted; God shifted quickly! I was able to stop sweating the small stuff enough to bring balance and unity to our marriage. God did something so indescribable in our marriage, and I know a lot of it has to do with The Power of Strategic and Effective prayers that continue to foster us in becoming one in Christ.

If you are reading this chapter and this resonates with you, I want to encourage you not to grow weary. I also want to urge you to stop focusing on your husband and start focusing on you. You work on becoming the most authentic version of who God created you to be and by doing that, your marriage and husband will follow suit. Talk less and do more. Allow your fruit to speak for you.

1 Peter 3:1-4 says "Wives, in the same way submit yourself to your own husbands so that, if any of them do not believe the word, they may be won over without the words by the behavior of their wives. When they see the purity and reverence of your lives. Your beauty should not come from outward adornment, such as elaborate hairstyles and wearing of gold jewelry or fine clothes. Rather it should be that of your inner self, the unfading beautify of a gentle and quiet spirit, which is of great worth in God's sight." This scripture was and still is my truth, and I stand on it until this day.

The Power of an Effective Prayer Life Reflection:

If you have been praying for your husband and marriage and your prayers are going unanswered; don't be discouraged. It can be a number of reasons why things have not shifted in your marriage and the best way to find out is to simply ask. We have not because we ask not and then sometimes when we do ask, we ask with doubt in our hearts or the wrong motives and still don't receive. There are no tricks to God and nothing spooky about him. The same way you desire a relationship with your husband, God desires one with you. If you want to have an effective prayer life and don't understand the whole prayer thing; I am extending myself to help you on this journey. Every Wednesday at 5:30AM EST, we host prayer via a conference line. We would love for you to join us and to tell a fellow Wife Who Wins. The conference number is 712-451-1083; access code: 457207#. Be on the lookout for the Wives Who Win 10 week Coaching Program, but in the meantime, *connect to our Wives Who Win Club via Facebook @ https://www.facebook.com/groups/273276863146874/.* ~~you can email us at officialwiveswho@gmail.com to get a head start on creating an effective prayer life.~~

Part II

Chapter 5
"The Dangers of a Single Minded Married Woman"

Did you know that marriage is the only relationship where you have the ability to choose your life long partner? All other lifelong relationships, for example, our parent, siblings, children, relatives, etc. are selected for us, but marriage is a personal choice. In choosing your lifelong partner, you have to realize that you are also choosing to allow that person to have rights to your life. You are opening up your entire world to this person, and they now have a say in what you do and how you do it on a very regular basis. *The basis of submission is giving someone authority to lead you.* Honestly, this was a difficult pill to swallow for me because as much as I wanted to be the perfect submissive wife *and one ~~who~~ that* was so open and honest with every part of me toward my husband, I wasn't. There were parts of me that I wanted to keep just for me due to my single-mindedness. There were certain financial and life decisions I wanted to keep just for me. There were decisions and things regarding my family and my son ~~who~~ *that* I wanted to keep just for me. I felt it was okay not to involve my husband in certain areas of my life because he didn't have a need to know or *needed to* be involved. I was a single mom and single (no husband) for a long time, and I felt quite confident and comfortable operating in this space. I was used to making my own money, and spending ~~my own money~~ *it* the way I wanted to spend it. I was used to making all the major decisions ~~in~~ *for* my life. I was okay with not including others in my business or getting their input, feedback or suggestions *as to* how I should do things because it was ME making things happen for me and my son. I had no accountability to others. I had a complete single-minded mindset. I didn't ask for permission because I did what I wanted. Because this was my mindset pre-wedding, it was still my mindset post wedding. I didn't renew my mind in this area.

I had no plans of changing the way I did some things because I didn't feel there was anything wrong with them but when you get married the game changes and the rules also.

As much *as* you hear about all the right things you need to do, changes you need to implement and adjustments you need to consider; it doesn't become so real until they start affecting areas in your life and marriage. A wise woman builds her house, but a foolish woman tears it down with her hands (her decisions and actions). You are a direct contributor to the wealth and health of your marriage; what and how you decide to contribute has to do with your mindset. One of the worst things you can do is act like you are single when you get married. When you don't allow your husband a say in any matters concerning your life with him and *the* children, regardless if they are his biologically *children* or not; you are setting yourself and marriage up for complete failure. I didn't know the effects of having a single mindset when married. I was the type of wife who would say inwardly you do you, and I do me — not us doing anything that would dishonor our marriage vows, but I didn't feel the need to be an open book because I lived a very private life for so long.

Unfortunately, the message displayed throughout many marriages today is that we are all individuals and it is okay to operate independently still — outside of, without or the absence of your husband when making certain decisions. This will only cause more chaos, confusion, and craziness in your marriage. When you make an intentional decision not to include your husband when making life choices, whether or not you feel as if he won't be impacted, it just sends a negative message about his purpose and existence in your life. It also sends a negative message to the children involved. He will feel left out; and your trust and respect for one another will also be affected. Sometimes the smallest matters need to be discussed because they can ultimately become big matters. Your ability to communicate with your husband, regardless of the magnitude of the matter, helps to build a healthy marriage. It has less to do with putting your husband in your business and more to do with building a strong friendship and companionship with someone who you choose to spend the rest of your life with. When I don't want to tell my husband certain things or if I feel they are insignificant, that is when I encourage myself that I should tell him. I want to continue becoming the type of wife that is so brutally honest and open with my husband so that any and all suspicion or things that are questionable are non-factors.

Many wives make the claim that their husbands are their best friends but in the same breath, they have held back aspects of themselves from their husbands. Typically, best friends talk about and share almost everything, if not everything.

There are three Dangers of a Single Minded Married Woman, and I want to share them with you.

1. **You are out of order.** When you are still operating as single minded woman in a marriage, you are outside the order of God and outside of the order or your convenant contract. As your husband submits to God, you must submit to Him. Your husband is the head, and the final decision maker. When you feel like you can do things without including him; you are out of order. Now you are running the risk of God not manifesting certain things in your life because you are out of order. That may be why God hasn't moved on some things you have been praying ~~on~~ for, *for* so long.

2. **You cause chaos, confusion, and corruption in your marriage**. Your marriage is doomed for destruction. When you continue to make single-minded decisions, go about living your single-minded lifestyle – you are doomed for destruction. When you are operating on any level of deceit or secrecy – this is single-mindedness. Having secret bank accounts or doing other things in secret because you feel like one day he can up and leave so you need to secure your life is not something I encourage nor is it scripture. Matthew 6:31-32 says "So do not worry, saying, "What shall we eat? Or what shall we drink? Or what shall wear. For the

pagans (unbelievers) run after all these things, and your heavenly Father knows that you need them." In essence, you don't have to have a secret bank account, a stash of cash, secret property, and other investments or do anything else in secret out of fear or deceit because God got you and your husband's future is secured. Lastly, marriage is a covenant contract until someone dies, so divorce or someone leaving the marriage prematurely (outside of death, dissertation or adultery) should not be the basis for any decisions made. Give no place to the devil — submit to God, resist the devil and he will flee from you.

3. **It is a bad example for your children**. If you are still operating in a single-minded mindset, what you are teaching your children is that it is okay to be single-minded and operate individually when you are married. You are teaching your children to lie, deceive others, and be rebellious. And daughters in particular, you are teaching them to disrespect those in authority and leadership by way of position. Your children will become what you are. Their marriage has a great percentage of turning out the same as yours. Even if you are not intentionally teaching them, they catch on and emulate certain behaviors and actions which stem from your mindset. Telling your children *"Do what I say, not what I Do'* does not work. Children will do what you do, so be mindful of what you are showing them by way of your actions and what you are teaching them for one day, they will become husbands and wives.

Understand this — what worked when you were single will not work once you get married. When you go into marriage with the same mindset you had as a single woman, your marriage will not stand a chance. I can't stress enough, through my conversations with wives to be and wives, that you have to go into marriage with a fresh mindset and perspective. It is something new and different, and for many, something you have never experienced before. The best thing you can do with your now or future husband is *to* sit down before or early on in your marriage and have a conversation about how things were handled when you were both single and together discuss and agree on how things will be done now that you are married.

The Dangers of Single Minded Married Woman Reflection:

I get it! You are Ms. Strong, Independent, Make things happen kinda gal. I was right there with you, but now that you are married, engaged or desiring marriage one day; things have to switch up a bit. It is never too late to work on renewing your mind so that your life and marriage will be transformed. Even if you didn't do this at the onset of marriage, it is okay and you can start right now. It isn't too late to change your mind and perspective of how you once thought and did things. Two are better than one, and if you and your husband can get on one accord in doing life together; your marriage will be better because of it. It is not about who is in charge, or one having more control or power over the other, but all about making it work for the greater good and well-being of the marriage while doing things differently, but just as effective. If this is your struggle, I got you girl, because I can totally relate and I am here to help. The Wives Who Win Coaching Program will be a great tool to help you in this area. Shoot me an email at offiicalwiveswhowin@gmail.com so we chat about it and see how you can sign up.

Chapter 6
Get a Life Outside of Your Husband

I can't stress enough how important it is to get a life outside of your husband. Too often, I speak to wives whose entire life and existence revolve around their husbands. They go along to get along and put all their time and energy into their husband and expect for him to do the same, but are disappointed when it's not reciprocated. These wives typically have very little to no friends and depend solely on their husband to meet their relationship needs. Many of these wives have not discovered their true self or purpose in life. They find it easier to hop on the bandwagon of life with their husband as opposed to discovering what God intended for them.

Beyond being a wife and mother, there is much more that God has for you. Too often women/wives are placed in certain categories which limit our ability to be great in other areas besides being a wife and mother. I am not saying there is no purpose in being a wife; mother, at home mother, etc., because I have stood in all those spaces at some time or another, but many women desire more and unsure of how to obtain more. I am talking to the wife who still has a dream, desire or hope to do some radical things in life. That wife who wants to use the gifts that God gave her to impact more than her household. I am talking to that wife who may have or are on the verge of losing her identity in her husband or children. She has found discontentment and complacency in her inner being because she fears what is ahead. She fears that she can't be great in other areas, as she is as wife or mother.

Please understand that your husband is neither equipped and, in some cases, don't desire to meet all your needs when it comes to your emotional, social, mental and spiritual needs. God made us relational creatures, and that means we are supposed to establish, build and grow other relationships outside of our husbands and children - those with our parents, children, friends, co-workers, etc. This is important because it lessens your desire to be super needy and dependent on one person; your husband, who is limited in his capacity to completely fulfill you. It bothers me when I hear wives say that their husbands complete them, and are their heart string, etc. What that says without actually saying it is your husband is all you need, and you can't live without him. Well, we know that isn't the case at all. I have often said this when speaking at various women events and even within our on/offline community that I can live without everything and everyone else, but I can't live without God. He is the only person who completes me and gives me reasons to live.

When you are unable to love life outside of your husband, this is a sign of insecurity, lack of faith in God and, in some cases, a complete turn off to your husband. This is also a sign of weakness to some degree; not poor in strength and feeble but a woman who lacks a strong mind, confidence, and wholeness within. Honey Chile, your husband isn't built that way, and although he may have tried filling those shoes in the past, I can almost guarantee you that he wouldn't mind you creating a healthy and productive life outside of him.

As wives, it is so important that as we work on building our marriages, we also work on building our individual lives, and building healthy external relationships with other people.

The happier and more fulfilled you are individually, the happier and more fulfilled your marriage will be as a result. Having a life outside of your husband does not take away from the marriage but it adds to it significantly. The more confident you become in who you are; the less you will depend on your husband to fill holes and voids that can only be filled via other relationships, including the one with God.

Also, this will take significant pressure off your husband when he wants to hang out with friends and have a guy's night out. He won't feel as if you are joined to his hip, or guilty for doing things that exclude you sometimes.

I have what I call the rule of three when it comes to relationships. **Number One**: You should have a relationship with God. **Number Two**: You should have a relationship with yourself. **Number Three**: You should have a relationship with others, including your husband. When you are operating in this realm of the horizontal relationships, some magical things happen within your own life. I can't stress enough how important it is for you to be productive and purposeful outside of your husband. Getting a productive life will not only increase your chance of inner happiness but it will almost guarantee happiness within your marriage.

Part of getting a productive life is establishing healthy friendships with a group of women who will be able to add and multiply to your life. Women who are like minded and who have similar aspirations and goals as you, particularly, as it relates to what you desire to achieve in life. The Bible says that bad company corrupts good character so that means good company eradicates bad character. If you have found it difficult to build healthy and meaningful friendships, the first thing I would encourage you to do is look within yourself. Don't be afraid, but dig deep to see what emotional or mental roadblocks preventing you from doing this. If you are finding it difficult or you don't feel like it is necessary to create a life outside of your husband, I want to share with you seven (7) benefits of how it will positively impact your marriage:

1. You will discover your true authentic self.
2. You will discover the purpose and assignment for your life.
3. You will build your confidence level and stand in your truth.
4. You will create internal happiness that you control, which in turn will benefit your marriage. You will no longer make others responsible for your happiness.
5. You will be able to start living and no longer existing.

6. You will learn to trust God more instead of putting your trust in others.

7. You will be a great example for your children, and give them something to look forward to when they get married.

Get A Life Reflection:

If you are guilty of being the needy wife, I want to challenge you to step outside of your comfort zone and get a life. Sista girl, your life does not revolve around your husband. He is one factor in your life, but not the only factor. You having a life of your own will be such a great reward and will help you to evolve into the truest version of yourself. You will be so much better as a result of it; your marriage will be healthier and more fulfilling.

One more thing, be sure you join the Wives Who Win Club via

Facebook @

https://www.facebook.com/groups/273276863146874/.

Chapter 7
Take Care & Keep It Sexy

Marriage is a major life change, and it is almost like your life changes overnight. The choices you made and life you lived on a day to day basis is no longer yours, but now includes the person you chose to spend the rest of your life with. How you take care of you should still be your top priority. Some would beg to differ and say that your husband should be your #1 priority, so allow me to un-package this for you. If you are so busy taking care of the rest of the world, then who is taking care of you? When you get tired, sick or overly exhausted then who will come to your rescue? Too often, we wives feel like we have to conquer the world around us. We put on the badge of honor as wife and mother of the year. We do this by putting extreme demands on our body. We go until we can't go anymore. We do until we can't do anymore and often find ourselves in a space where we can't be there for ourselves the way we need to. This often results to letting you go physically. Where you once put in the time, energy and money to keep yourself looking, smelling and feeling good; you have placed most of that on the backburner. That now becomes a lesser priority for you, and in turn, your husband suffers as well.

Many wives loose motivation in the upkeep department. Some feel like because they have achieved the ultimate goal of marriage, there is no need to put their best foot forward anymore. I beg to differ and make the argument that what you did to get your husband, you should continue doing to keep your husband. Men are visual creatures, and his first attraction to you was not because you are smart or spiritual. During the introduction phase, he sees your exterior before he gets to know deeper parts of you. His first impression was your looks. That is what caught his eye; the extra benefits and extremities of you are what captured his heart. In knowing that; you should be just as intentional as you were before marriage to take care of yourself during the marriage. I know the dynamics change in marriage, however, you have to make this a priority in the same way you make other things a priority. Don't lose momentum or motivation in looking good for you first and then your husband. I said for you first, because, again, you don't want to lose yourself in your husband's world and only do it for him because it will seem like more of a task or obligation and down the road of your marriage, you will resent him. Do it because this is who you have always been. You have always taken pride in caring for you and looking sexy but modestly. Do it because you are confident in who you are. Do it because you are happy with you and want to share your happiness with the world in how you show up. Do it because you want to, and because you can.

Your ability to love yourself shows up in how you treat yourself, and treating yourself well has **to do with how you take care of you. Treat yourself to spa days, shopping sprees, weekend trips or whatever that looks like for you and is within your budget. Part of doing these things is so you don't lose yourself or forget your self-wor**th and value. When you take care of you, it shows others how to take care of you as well.

To my wives who are mothers and especially to young children; don't become so overwhelmed and lost in raising your children that you forget about you and hubby. Children are seasonal, and as a mother, you should do everything you can to care for them and raise them to be outstanding people but you don't have to sacrifice ALL of you or your marriage in the process. Your husband is your first priority, and your children come second (after your husband). Your husband being your priority has a lot to do with how you show up for him as well. We will talk more about priorities in a later chapter. Your husband deserves parts of you in the same way your children does, and I know it can be quite the balancing act, but it is workable.

You will hear me say time and time again that your ability to have a healthy and happy marriage has to do with you. Taking care of you has to do with you and your level of happiness and confidence before marriage. When you get married, things evolve and get better; they should not dissolve or get worst. That is why I express strongly to wives to continue building your self-esteem and confidence — discover who you are so this person will show up in your marriage more often than not. Doing these things will bring out that sexy side of you and focus less on your flaws and blemishes and more on the incredible person you are. It will help you to be bold in standing in your true self so when you put on that outfit or decide to wear that exotic hairstyle, you are confident. Your confidence screams sexy very loudly to your husband. Confidence is one of the things that turns your husband on and increases the attraction level he has for you. The more confident you are, the more in tune he is with you.

I encourage you to check in with your husband every now and again to test the temperature of your sexiness. Sometimes we become too comfortable in wearing the nightly head wraps and oversized, mismatched pajamas to bed every night and if your husband is like mine and doesn't say anything; you feel like it is okay. Let me share something with you; just because he may not say anything verbally, he may be saying it non-verbally or feeling it, but haven't expressed it. I know for me, I get certain responses from my husband when I do certain things like wear matching pajamas, lingerie or take some time to put on some good smelling lotion or perfume. He is more frisky, compliments more and more attentive and I like that. I feel better when I look better going to bed or in public. This goes back to confidence and in taking pride in how you look in and outside of the house. There are days I don't feel sexy for one reason or another but in those days, I try to put on my best and smell my best, and it stimulates the sexy nature within, which is quite alright, wives. If your husband enjoys lingerie, go stock up on some and plan to wear it twice a week. If he enjoys you smelling good; be intentional about putting a dab of his favorite scents on before bed; if he likes your hair a certain way, be nicel and wear it for a period of time. This goes for certain clothing, etc. You know your husband, and you know what he likes, and you should make that a priority at times. Like me, I change hairstyles like the weather and some styles my husband loves, while others he is not fond of, but I love to change it up a bit. I will wear what he likes sometimes and what I like sometimes and it works. One thing about my husband though is that he will buy me what he likes and I have no problem at all with that, because I trust him and he chooses the best for me as he would for himself. If you have no clue what your husband likes, ask him and be willing and open to make some adjustments.

Take Care & Keep it Sexy Reflection:

If taking care of you is one of your struggles; then I want to challenge you to take some time out for you this week. If you need to get a babysitter, readjust your schedule or whatever it takes; do it. No more excuses that your husband and children need you. I am not negating the fact that they do, but you need you as well, and you have to make sure you are not taking care of others from an empty cup.

If the sexiness is diminishing in your life and this chapter brought clarity and confirmation regarding what you need to do in that department, I challenge you to start working on that this week as well. If there are some other issues like weight, and low self-esteem preventing you from keeping it sexy; there are things you can do to get to your overall size, healthy and build your self-esteem. You are not in this alone and I am willing to bet that there are hundreds of wives, if not thousands, who feel the way you feel and have given up on trying to keep it sexy. I encourage you to connect with our online Wives Who Win community via Facebook **@facebook.com/**

wiveswhowin. I also encourage you to email us at officialwiveswhowin@gmail.com so we can send you some more information on our 10 Step-Wives Who Win Coaching Program that will help support you in this area.

PART III

Chapter 8
After the Big Day "Stay Committed to Your Marriage"

Too often, couples get married and have a false sense of hope and expectation for their marriage relationship. That leads to a place of unhappiness and discontentment with the relationship itself or your partner. It is the trick of the enemy to find small entry ways into your union so you will second guess your decision or even your partner. He wants you to feel as if your marriage will not work regardless of how hard you try.

For a long time, I would hear people say that God will send you a man or woman of God, but the longer I live and the wiser I become in my God-relationship, I am confident that God allows you to choose your mate and if you allow Him to be the center of it, he will bless your marriage tremendously. Just because God is the center of your marriage; that does not mean you will not face adversity. What that does mean is that you face it together and with God leading the way.

On the contrary, if you choose your mate and remove God out of the equation, it will be very hard for him to bless something He has no access to. God will never force His way into your life or marriage even if things are not going as planned. Faith is believing and asking God to move on your behalf, not sitting back with your hands folded expecting Him to do something about your situation because He is God.

Having been married for almost five years, I know that marriage is an investment. I am not saying that to be cliché but I am saying that because I believe people don't understand the depth of a relationship or marriage and what it takes to stay together, stay committed and stay happy. I have witnessed so many marriages where people are together, but they are far from being happy.

Couples have mastered commitment (sticking and staying) with one another, while they are miserable. God's desire is not for you to be miserable or discontent in your covenant relationship. If you are married, and you are finding yourself in any of these spaces, it is time for you to go back to the drawing board of your marriage to see what/how you can reposition yourself and your mind, so that true happiness is evident in your marriage.

What I have discovered even in my marriage are three (3) tools that will help you to stay committed to your covenant relationship. You can argue that it takes more than that and your argument is valid, but today, I will share with you only three (3).

The first tool is **Communication**: How many times do we hear this but yet so many struggle with communicating effectively with their spouses? Healthy and effective communication will break the barriers in your marriage; prevent division and discord, and any other negative attribute that will try to creep into the marriage relationship. Too many marriages fall apart because couples cannot or refuse to communicate effectively with one another. Instead of trying to resolve the issue as one, couples often point the finger at the other person for them to feel as if they are off the hook for whatever the issue is. It is only when you learn how to efficiently and consistently communicate with your partner, not identifying anyone to blame, but both taking part in the reason why the issue exists and together coming up with a solution to resolve.

The second tool to staying committed to your covenant relationship is **Connection:** You have to connect with one another on a regular basis. I am talking about sex, intimacy, and conversation and otherwise. Connection is critical. I know all about the weight of the world and the busyness of life and how that can cause disconnection. My hubby and I have those same challenges. Sometimes you give so much to other things; and give less to your partner. It isn't right, but it is the reality. So how do you make it right? By being intentional in staying connected! Sharing common space does not equate to having a connection. A connection is when both parties are engaged mind, body, and spirit with one another at any given time. It is the enemies job to steal, kill and destroy, especially marriages, so when you allow yourself to become disconnected in any of those aspects, that is a sure way for the enemy to come in and attempt to separate you two in mind, body, or spirit or all three.

Here are a few ways you can stay connected:

Plan date nights weekly or bi-weekly; plan to spend intimate time together. Plan to engage in intellectual and meaningful conversations together. Plan to get in touch with one another on a deeper level and plan to have sex, and enjoy it.

The third way you can stay committed to your covenant relationship is **Consistency**. I despise people who are inconsistent. Inconsistency tells me I cannot count on you; I cannot trust you and I cannot rely on you.

In a marriage, sometimes it is difficult to be consistent because issues arise, events happen, moods change, and feelings and emotions will have you not wanting to be consistent in displaying love and respect toward your husband. I am here to tell you that when you are able to remain consistent in how you treat your husband and how you treat yourself; how you love your husband and how you submit one to another, you will see that your marriage will continue to grow and prosper each and every single day. Consistency allows love to abound over every negative thing that may be going on or have happened in your marriage. The only way you can stay consistent in your marriage relationship is when you stay consistent in your God relationship. I guarantee you that if you use these three tools in your marriage, you will find great joy in staying committed in your covenant relationship.

After the Big Day "Stay Committed to Your Marriage" Reflection:

If this is a struggle for you, I want to encourage you to go back to the Word of God and to see how all three of these tools were exemplified throughout scripture in the Apostle Paul's life, in the life of Jesus and in their relationship to the church (body of Christ). If you would like to learn more about staying committed to your marriage and need support in this area, please feel free to email us at officialwiveswhowin@gmail.com. Our 10 Step-Wives Who Win Coaching Program would be a great place to start. Be sure you are connected to our Facebook page **@facebook.com/wiveswhowin** for daily inspiration and motivational post that will lead to a transformation in your marriage.

Chapter 9
What Does Love Got to Do With It?
"Four Types of Love"

Did you know that there are four types of love? Well, I didn't know until a few years ago when I started researching love. We often equate love to that mushy feeling that one gets when they care about someone who means a great deal to them. I know for a long time I misapplied and misappropriate love and gave to others what I felt they deserved; nothing more and nothing less. When it came to my marriage, I thought surely I had mastered my love walk toward others but the lack thereof showed up in my marriage. I had great intentions and strongly felt that the feelings I had for my husband were enough to sustain and grow our marriage.

The four types of love are displayed differently given the type of relationship you have with another person. I will share all four, but only focus on the few that will help sustain and grow the marriage. I once heard someone say that your true love walk is tested with those you are closest to. Your faith in God is also tested by the demonstration of your ability to love others even when they don't seem loveable. The ability to receive love the right way is a woman's strongest desire, but sometimes our ability to return that love is not always reciprocated. Quite honestly, our love in marriage is sometimes conditional and based on our husband's behavior and attitude toward us, at least mine was. Love is an action word, and at any time you find yourself not wanting to do, because of the behavior and attitude of someone else, you should question your love or ability to express love toward that person. I have heard women say that they act and do certain things because of their husband's behavior and attitude, but your response or reaction to your husband has little to do with him and more to do with you — your true self-being revealed and your lack of demonstrating unconditional love.

The Four Types of Love are: Agape, Philia, Eros, and Storge.

-Agape (pronounced a-gah-pee) meaning divine, unconditional, self-sacrificing love; the kind of love God says we should have for each other — love without emotions, conditions, feeling, non-judgmental and is non-circumstantial.

-Philia/Phileo: means close friendships or brotherly love in Greek. This is the love we would have for our friends or sisters/brothers in Christ. Strong emotional connection between friends. You can agape your enemies, but you cannot phileo them.

-Eros: Physical, sensual love between a husband and wife (sexual).

-Storge: family love, the bond among parents and siblings, children, etc.

Now that you know the four types of love and have a brief understanding of how they are expressed, it should be pretty clear that each of them should be present in a marriage, but for these purposes we will focus more on Agape. Expressing Agape love was the most challenging for me in my marriage early on. As I alluded to earlier, my love was conditional and circumstantial based on what my husband may have said or did or did not say or do. If I can bare my truth with you; I was controlling and judgmental, and this showed up in my marriage. When I felt like my husband wasn't doing something the way it needed to be done, I would judge him and attempt to control the situation so that I got the results I wanted. I had no concern for what he wanted.

One thing I have learned during the course of my marriage is your feelings will leave you disappointed and feeling lonely many days. Marriage is not based on emotions and feelings or any of the other love types alone. You can have a sexual connection with your husband, and not have any other connection and that will not sustain your marriage. You can love him like a brother but even brothers/siblings turn their back on each other. Proverbs 18:24 says even a friend stick closer to you than a brother. Your love toward your husband has to be more than an emotional fix. When the going gets tough and the tough gets going, you need something that will help your marriage push past any ambiguity or adversity. Agape love allows you to see your husband through God's lenses and not in his natural state. It allows you to look past all his faults and flaws and see him as God's son, not just the man you married. It allows you to stop being judgmental toward him and intentionally display grace toward him because, like you, he deserves the gift of grace.

When I began to demonstrate Agape love in my marriage, and I mean truly demonstrate — it took our marriage to a totally different level. My expectations for my husband lessened, not in a bad way, but it was then I truly appreciated his limitations in the flesh and started to rely on and press in on his spiritual ability to love me unconditional. There is no good thing that dwells in the flesh, and my husband's ability to love me and me him in the flesh is so very limited. Fleshly love will constantly be guided and manipulated by how one treats the other and it is circumstantial. Fleshly love will choose feelings every time and when feelings don't feel the way we want or need; we will choose not to love in what we do or say.

My husband and I discovered that choosing to love via our Faith (Agape) rather than our Feelings (Eros, Storge or Phillia) was one of the anecdotes to Winning in your Marriage God's Way.

What Does Love Got to Do With It? "Four Types of Love Reflection:

Has loving your husband conditionally and circumstantially been an issue for you? It sounds good to say that we love our husbands unconditionally, but the true test of our love is when conditions and circumstances arise. Let's break down 1 Corinthians 13:4-7 to check your love temperature. This is how I measure my love, not only toward my husband, but others and I can tell you, it is pretty dead on, and I have found myself reevaluating my love.

Vs. 4 Love is patient and kind. (Are you always patient and kind toward your husband?) Love is not jealous or boastful or proud. (Have you found yourself jealous, boastful or proud regarding something your husband did, say or did not say or do during the course of your marriage?)

Vs.5 Love is not rude. It does not demand its own way. It is not irritable, and it keeps no record of being wrong. (I failed miserably on this one) How about you? Listen, we are not doing this to point out your flaws, but so that you identify the areas in your marriage that need work, so you can be intentional about doing the work to strengthen the health of your marriage.

Vs. 6 Love does not rejoice about injustice, but rejoices whenever the truth wins out. (Have you been a hidden hater in your husband's life when something didn't work out for him? If he loses at life, you lose as well. Think about it!)

Vs. 7. Love never gives up, never loses faith, is always hopeful, and endures through every circumstance. (I know I have been in the position of wanting to give up, I have lost faith, I was not always hopeful, and Lord knows I felt endurance was a punishment. So now it is time to bare your truth. What do you need to demonstrate Agape love toward your husband? How can I help you on this

Love Journey, so it is demonstrated daily and in every circumstance of your marriage?)

We have an online Wives Who Win *Club* community via Facebook @~~facebook.com/wiveswhowin~~ *https://www.facebook.com/groups/273276863146874/.* We have insurmountable amount of women waiting to embrace you and to lock elbow with you on your Love Journey. I also encourage you to email us at officialwiveswhowin@gmail.com so we can send you some more information on our 10 Step-Wives Who Win Coaching Program that will help support you in this area of Love.

Chapter 10
Sex is Overrated

I thought once I got married, and no longer living a life of fornication and sexual immorality, that my sexual appetite would have been through the roof. But in reality, it wasn't, and honestly, I found myself wanting sex less in marriage than when I was in the world. I found myself exhausted most days, filling up my life with tasks, projects, work, etc., and not including or even desiring a space for sex. For the life of me, I couldn't figure out what was going on with my mind or body. It was like my sex button was turned off for good. I know before I got married, I asked God to help me control the strong desire to prevent fornication and other sexual immoral activity, but now I was married and sex was now spiritually legal.

A few things were going on, more so in the spiritual than in the natural but of course, it affected my natural being. Romans 12:1-2 says, *I beseech (plead) therefore, brethren, by the mercies of God, that ye present your bodies as a living sacrifice, holy, acceptable unto God, which is your reasonable service. And be not conformed to this world: but be ye transformed by the renewing of your mind, that ye may prove what is the pleasing, perfect will of God.* I had gotten so comfortable in living this scripture before marriage, and I was determined not to dishonor God. I embedded thoughts in my mind about sex and some thoughts screamed impurity, lust and unclean due to my past life of sexual immorality. Although, I knew God forgave me, redeemed and restored me; parts of me still walked in condemnation. I was still beating myself up for not honoring God in my past life when I knew better and especially when I gave my life to Him. I would think about all the times I messed up; all the times I hurt Him and those who loved me, because of the careless decisions I made to have pre-marital sex. I knew that this thinking was off, but the reason why it was there is that I needed to do what vs. 2 says and renew my mind. This couldn't be a one-time thing, but I had to renew my mind constantly and daily to accept that I was forgiven; my past was no longer a factor and that God honored sexual fulfillment in the context of marriage.

God instructed us to remain pure because he understood how sexual immoral behavior/activity would affect our lives and relationships. He knew the cost of misusing our bodies and wanted to prevent us from living a life of heartache, pain, and regret. Proverbs 5:18 says, *May your fountain be blessed, and may you rejoice in the wife of your youth.* God's desire is for us to remain abstinent until marriage and once we find the one, then marry until death do us part. In the meantime, we are to honor God only with our bodies according to 1 Corinthians 6:19-20 *"Do you not know that your bodies are temples of the Holy Spirit, who is in you, whom you have received from God? You are not your own; you were bought at a price. Therefore honor God with your bodies."*

Guilt, shame, embarrassment and disappointment of my past ripped through my mind and attempted to cut through my marriage, but I was determined to do something about it. Not that I wanted us to be like two uncontrolled sex maniacs, but we both desired a healthy sex and intimacy life; one that pleased us naturally and honored God spiritually. I understood exactly what was going on with me; so I began to seek answers. I searched the Word, and then I invested in materials on sex and marriage. This was not so much about my husband as it was about me. Although, we didn't intend to withhold from one another, in the same breath, it wasn't a priority, and it needed to be. I placed this part of my marriage on the altar of God's heart and prayed/fasted that He strengthen this area and complete the work within me. It was and will always be my desire to please my husband, and I needed to make sure that nothing (including myself and old thoughts) would be a deterrent from doing that.

I thank God for my husband, for having such a loving heart and a listening ear, even when I didn't verbally express myself, but he still understood. I knew that sex alone couldn't sustain our marriage but that it was a very vital part of it and it was needed to connect with one another on a much deeper level. Sex and intimacy are needed for the health of the marriage. It is another piece to the puzzle to Winning in your Marriage God's Way. It is a sum part of the whole picture of marriage. The marriage bed is holy and undefiled and should be honored by all. The marriage bed should be kept pure, for God will judge the adulterer and all the sexually immoral. We are to remain faithful to one another and never withhold sex or intimacy physically, emotionally or mentally.

Sex is Over-Rated Reflection:

The marriage bed is consecrated and unpolluted. Once God cleanses you of all your sins and unrighteous behavior; then that settles it. There is no condemnation to those who are in Christ Jesus. If you are feeling condemned about your past life and it is affecting your sexual engagement with your husband, I encourage you to place it on the altar of God's heart. If you are finding your old sexual ways and habits being a roadblock in your marriage, lay it on the altar. If sex is leading your marriage, then that is a lust issue, and lust will affect the health of your marriage.

"For everything in the world, the lust of the flesh, the lust of the eyes, and the pride of life, comes not from the Father, but from the world" -1 John 2:16.

Get to the root of the sex issue in your marriage and be kind and willing enough to please one another. Too little or too much is something that you and your husband need to talk about and agree on. Always keep the other in mind but don't lose yourself in the process. If you need additional resources or support in this area, email us at officialwiveswhowin@gmail.com and put in the subject line "Sex is Overrated Reflection."

Chapter 11
Prioritizing Priorities (Blend ed Family Blues)

And the Lord God said, "It is not good for the man to be alone. I will make a helper suitable for him." So the Lord God caused the man to fall into a deep sleep; and while he was sleeping, He took one of the man's ribs and closed up the place with flesh. Then the Lord God made a woman from the rib (side) he had taken out of the man, and he brought her to the man. (Gen 2:18, 21 22)

There is quite the controversial issue. Who is considered a **priority**; in particular within a blended family. Fact: Step-families and second families are more common today than ever. Fact: The divorce rate for second marriages, when only one partner has children, is over 65 percent. When both partners have children, the rate rises to 70 percent (Slayer-Giles, 2011).

The conversation here then shifts from why are the odds so against marriages to why are the odds so against blended families? As I was doing some reading and researching on this topic; I found some pretty interesting things. Having a blended family of my own, I was able to totally relate to what I call *"Day 1 Challenges"* of a blended family. What I often share with single moms who desire to get married is that the dynamics of their family unit will be different from day 1; not bad but just different. I then tell them the best way to deal with different is to simply accept it as your normal and that they are in control of making the very best of it. When I first got married, I did not understand this concept or I did not accept this concept of my family dynamics being different. I was determined to force my family to be structured a certain way despite the dynamics of what was my reality. I knew what the divine order was according to the Word — God, Marriage, Family (includes children), but I didn't necessarily implement or acknowledge that order in many cases early on in my marriage.

I was a single mom for 16 years before I got married. My son and I have always (still do) had a great, close knitted relationship, and it was great, as long as it was just him and me. Ladies, having a male friend or boyfriend that come over often and even spend the night from time to time is entirely different than getting married. I had certain expectations of how I wanted my family to reflect and instead of me conveying those expectations to my husband before our wedding; I tried to force my expectations on him after the fact. I had a family with my son before I had an actual family with all three of us, so I was used to doing things a certain way and I already pre-established in my mind what that would look like long term. I hear women say a lot of the time *"Well if he loves me; then he has to love my child (ren) in the same way."* What if he doesn't even like your children; love will be far from that or even falsified to win or keep you. The reason I say that is because you and your husband are establishing a different love and bond with each other, so the love he has for you won't necessarily be the love he has for your child(ren) from day one; however, he can choose to love them in his own way without you trying to force feed him your child(ren). It is like trying to wear a size 5 shoe when you were a size 9. As painful as it is; you can't force things to happen in your way and on your terms. It will take time and in fact, sometimes it can take years for the step-father to establish a healthy, loving and meaningful relationship and friendship with the child (ren) as in the step-mother if you hold that space. Raising someone else's child can be very confusing and difficult and it takes a lot of work to develop these types of relationships.

Because my son and I were a family of two for so long; I struggled with prioritizing priorities when I got married. Honestly, I did not know how. This situation was so different and I found myself trying to wiggle my way through and hoping for the best. I feared that if I made my marriage a priority; my relationship with my son would suffer and if I made my son a priority; my marriage would suffer. These are real life struggles that many mom/wives are dealing with today and they are not talked about enough. We push these topics aside or under a rug somewhere and focus too much on the surface; it is time to remove the carpet and deal with what is underneath. For a long time, I was between a rock and a hard place when it came to decision making, showing love and affection, choosing one over the other; so I did what I thought was best and I separated our relationships. On one hand, I had a relationship with my son, and on the other hand, I had a relationship with my husband, and I didn't allow those relationships to cross or co-mingle. I didn't often include my husband with my son's affairs, and I didn't often include my son with my husband affairs.

Let me tell you what was wrong with that; I created division in my home. The very thing that I was trying to avoid; I created. How crazy was that? All because I didn't know and I was trying to be in control of the situation. I never wanted my son to feel like he came after my husband (because of our long-established bond) and I never wanted my husband to feel like he came after my son (because of our newly formed relationship and life-long commitment). I know the struggle is real and that is why I felt this chapter was necessary. For some of you, this is the reason why you are not winning in your marriage. I hear women say things like their children are their world, and no one will ever come before their children, and in some cases, women have boldly told their husbands in front of the children that their children will always be number one. How rude and outright disrespectful and no wonder the craziness in those marriages continue. You can, and sometimes will, deal with all sorts of crazy and ambiguity in your family dynamic, but it is the parents (the adults in the relationship) responsibility to stand and work together through all of it and at no time should the biological parent of the child(ren) side with the child(ren) and leave the step parent feeling lonely and left out of the family dynamic.

I had to learn this and if you truly desire to be a Wife Who Wins and you have children from a previous relationship or even children with your current husband; you have to prioritize priorities. Your husband should never feel like the outsider of his family and I know sometimes we can make them feel this way, and it isn't always intentional but sometimes a natural response to us *"protecting"* our seeds. It is good to check in every now and again to see how everything is flowing in your family unit. In checking in, make sure you are not comparing your family dynamics to others; accept and own your truth as a blended or different family type; don't compete with the Jones or Browns in trying to establish a family dynamic like them. Don't complain about your husband and child (ren) relationship, but be grateful that they have a relationship and working toward building a better or closer one and don't interfere. These are things I had to learn and continue to learn and display within my own family. I had to work on being consistent, not only in what I said but in what I did in prioritizing priorities.

My husband, after God, will always be my priority. Now situational things may call for my son to be a priority at that moment. However, that is the exception and not the rule. Wives, get on and stay on the same page with your husband and show your children by way of how you and your husband's interact that you both are inseparable and in agreement with each other. If there are any disagreements, don't disagree with your husband in front of the child(ren). This is interpreted as disrespect, and it can send mix messages to the children if you are often bucking and disagreeing with his decisions. Not only will this give the children a free pass to treat him like this, but they will treat others in authority the same way. Children know and do play parents against one another, but you have to be intentional in prioritizing priorities. Here are a few things that helped me along the way in prioritizing priorities and I know will help you as well:

1. **Confront and deal with family conflict in a healthy manner.** If an issue is brought before the family; resolve it in front of the family. Children will handle conflict in the way they are taught or caught. If disagreements arise; handle these between you and your husband. Once it is handled, include the children so they can see that mom and dad are on the same page and although there was a disagreement; they are settling the issue and working through it together. In the long-term this will show the children how to handle conflict effectively.

2. **Be clear with your husband and child(ren) that your marriage is a priority.** The child(ren) should know that the marriage is the priority and that the marriage, not the children, drive the family unit. The children are an extension of the marriage, whether biological or step children.

3. **Never take sides with the child (ren) in front of your husband, even when you don't agree with him or his approach to something.**

4. **Biblically share with your child (ren) why your husband/marriage is a priority over them.**

5. **Create a healthy and safe environment for topics to be shared and try to remain unbiased**

and, sometimes, emotionally detached when needed.

These are just some of the ways that keep me winning in my marriage. My marriage is my priority, as it should be yours as well, and when you make this clear and your truth; extraordinary things within your dynamic family unit will begin to happen. I am a living witness.

Prioritizing Priorities (Blended Family Blues Reflection):

Have you been guilty of putting your husband on the backburner? Does he feels like a mere afterthought in the marriage and often put to the side instead, and not encouraged to be a part of much less lead family discussions and decisions? Do you often take sides with the children because they are your children and you want to make sure they don't turn against you? If you have answered yes to any of these or had to think long and hard; I can tell you that you are on the road to building a permanent wall between you and your husband. Too many wives make the mistake of doing this and when the children grow up and move out/away (which they will); they feel as if they have married complete strangers. The love and respect in the marriage was lost long ago. If you have been guilty of misplaced priorities in your marriage; there is some good news – you have the power to turn things around. Yep, it is within your sole power to make a difference starting today. If I were you; I would start with jotting down some ways how you can start changing the dynamics or undoing what you have done for how many months or years. Once you have done that; ask God to help you come to grips with the position He has placed your husband in within the home.

The book of Ephesians; in particular Chapters 4 & 5, will help you with this. Also, pray and ask God to soften your husband's heart toward you and the children where it has become hardened and perhaps broken. Once you have done that; it is time to have that conversation with your husband and face the truth and nothing but the truth. If there is some drawback; go back to the drawing board to see what else is there that is causing you to go against the divine order of God.

Our 10 Week Wives Who Win Coaching Program is designed to help you tear down some internal barriers that are causing division and dysfunction in your marriage. If this chapter resonated with you; I know that the coaching program would be a great fit. Email us at officialwiveswhowin@gmail.com to sign up and learn more.

PART IV

Chapter 12
Fighting Fair (Healthy Conflict)

I can hear my granny Myrtices saying *"A girl should be seen and now heard."* That was her way of telling me I had a mouth problem, meaning, I talked too much and I didn't know how to gently craft my words to avoid hurting someone feelings. This was the norm growing up. I was never too much of a physical fighter, but I certainly could win an argument of any size and with whatever gender. I enjoy a great debate but sometimes I tend to take over the debate. I had a way with words, and if you attacked me; you had better be ready for whatever came next. I used this same system when I was in an abusive relationship. Because I was weaker in stature physically; I didn't use my hands as a weapon, but I certainly used my mouth. I guess it is safe to say that for a long time I did not know how to fight fair and I used my tongue of mass destruction when I felt others were being unloving, unkind, disrespectful or rude toward me. I used my tongue to tear down rather than to build up and the more I felt attacked; the more aggressive I became with my words. The tongue is small, but a very powerful force. In fact, James 3:1-12 had this to say about the tongue:

Controlling the Tongue

"Dear brothers and sisters, not many of you should become teachers in the church, for we who teach will be judged more strictly. Indeed, we all make many mistakes.

For if we could control our tongues, we would be perfect and could also control ourselves in every other way. We can make a large horse go wherever we want by means of a small bit in its mouth. And a small rudder makes a huge ship turn wherever the pilot chooses to go, even though the winds are strong. In the same way, the tongue is a small thing that makes grand speeches. But a tiny spark can set a great forest on fire. And among all the parts of the body, the tongue is a flame of fire. It is a whole world of wickedness, corrupting your entire body. It can set your whole life on fire, for it is set on fire by hell itself. People can tame all kinds of animals, birds, reptiles, and fish, but no one can tame the tongue. It is restless and evil, full of deadly poison. Sometimes it praises our Lord and Father, and sometimes it curses those who have been made in the image of God. And so blessing and cursing come pouring out of the same mouth. Surely, my brothers and sisters, this is not right! Does a spring of water bubble out with both fresh water and bitter water? Does a fig tree produce olives, or a grapevine produce figs? No, and you can't draw fresh water from a salty spring."

Your inability to control your tongue will cause you to get into arguments that could have been avoided; magnify disagreements that should have been simple in nature; break apart relationships; destroy others character and self-worth all because you are trying to win the argument. As women, we typically live in a Win Win world, whereas men understand and live in a Win or Lose world. For this reason, at times, it causes us to ignore the bigger picture and focus more on ourselves and how we feel at the moment. I didn't say it, but you were probably thinking it. Yes, we can be a bit emotional at times and our emotions can cause our tongues to spiral out of control. I know this was my case - in addition to the fact that I was used to fighting with my mouth; I wanted to win every argument and get to the bottom of every disagreement, but unfortunately, sometimes that caused us to fight unfairly. Both my husband and I wanted to get to the bottom of the problem, but we had a different way of getting to the bottom, and saw the bottom totally different. Whereas I wanted to go on and on until I felt emotionally satisfied; he wanted to create a divergent; stay focused on the issue, and then be over it, never to return. Well that did not work for me and I made it known.

Wives; your husband is your life long partner and if you need to get along with anyone; it would be him. Some things are non-negotiable, but most things are! I believe that couples should disagree and have heated fellowship moments (arguments), but it should not be at the expense of tearing the other person down.

Healthy conflict contributes to the overall health of the marriage. Men and Women are two different people so you will not always agree, and you have two very different personalities, so how you handle things and the lenses you see the world and situations through are totally different. Dr. Emerson Eggerichs puts it like this "Women see through pink sunglasses and hear with pink hearing aids, while men see through blue sunglasses and hear with blue hearing aids. In other words, women and men are very different." We have to accept that truth. Disagreeing is not about pointing out who is right or wrong, but it is simply a reflection of your personality. If God made us both the exact same, then one of us would be unnecessary. I discovered that truth; learned to accept and respect my husband's difference of opinions more, and chose to fight fair. I also had to do some internal work so I could use my words to build up rather than tear down, even when I didn't agree with what was being said, or how it was being said. I wrote an entire book on affirmations to help me Speak Differently. It is entitled Speak Life "31 Powerful Affirmations That Will Change Your Life". You can order it here:

https://www.amazon.com/Speak-Life-Powerful-Affirmations-Change/dp/1535294418

There is no way to avoid conflict, but you can choose healthy conflict, and in fact, healthy conflict within your marriage can help your marriage grow deeper in intimacy. It will help you appreciate one another more and accept that although you have differences in opinions; that alone can help build a healthier and happier marriage. You won't always have to see or do things one way, but you will have options to choose from. When handling conflict; there are some things that should be avoided and boundaries that need to be established when differences of opinions arise. At no time should you leave one another upset or overly angry, but agree to disagree, and if needed; table the issue and deal with it at a later time. Boundaries would include some below the belt rules in staying away from things you know about each other's past or present that you know will trigger them. Be intentional about keeping the peace, not in stirring up strife.

Fighting Fair (Healthy Conflict) Reflection:

It is no secret that I did not know how to fight fair in my marriage, and this caused my husband and I to be at odds with one another. Instead of me waiting on him to make every situation better; I took matters into my own hands. I took the high road and owned up to my truth and decided to do things differently. He was reacting off me and I was off him so instead of continuing on the crazy cycle, as Dr. Emerson Eggerichs refers to it; I got off and started to contribute to the energizing cycle. Funny thing is that I was operating in this prior to any knowledge of such cycles existed.

If you and your husband have been fighting unfair; I am going to challenge you to take the high road. Since you are the one who invested in this book; that tells me you are ready to WIN in your marriage and because this chapter is screaming in your ear; it is time to do something about it starting today. If you are like me and had some other issues that were contributing to your behavior; we need to have a conversation beyond this book. Email us at officialwiveswhowin@gmail.com to schedule your FREE 1-on-1 session.

Chapter 13
Mastering Emotions (Avoiding the Craziness & Chaos)

I am embarrassed to say that I sucked at mastering my emotions and, early on in my marriage, my husband was so kind (sarcastic smile) in letting me know how emotional I was. Although his timing and way of telling me couldn't have been more wrong; he was telling the truth. Everything I did not like, I reacted to it or him to say the least. I just had to get it out because keeping it in made me feel like I was trapped and weak as if I was giving up my authority. I wasn't a crier or dramatic queen but I had a lack of self-control when it came to when, how or why I expressed myself the way I did, and I was oversensitive and felt that my husband was not sensitive enough. I wanted to talk and work through everything and that would exasperate him and when I saw that; I would get offended and my feelings would be hurt. I would hold onto a word, statement or anything my husband said and would just dwell on it for hours, days or even weeks. I would allow my emotions to take me on a whirlwind and this created emotional distance in my marriage. Whereas my husband thought I was dramatic; I was merely trying to prove a point and I also wanted to work through my emotions. Ladies, it is okay to work through your feelings but at no given time should it be a lasting process that will create any distance between you and your husband.

The earlier parts of my 20s and early 30s, I focused more on my spiritual growth and development. I didn't pay too much attention to my personal growth and development because I felt that this would fall into place as I grew spiritually. This couldn't be further from the truth, and in fact, my spiritual growth and development caused me to mask my lack of personal growth and development. I was spiritually equipped and ready for marriage, but personally, I still had a lot of work to do, but I, not my husband or anyone else, had come to grips with this and made a decision to work on me, even after I got married. Marriage isn't the anecdote for anything, but it is a sure way to test your ability to do life successfully with someone else and for you to have a successful marriage; your personal life has to demonstrate success. I am not talking about tangible success here, but intangible.

There are so many resources available that will help you test your emotional IQ and master your emotions, and I have to say that it works. These resources will help you get to the root of your emotional issues. Emotions are mere energy; they are changed or aroused at any given moment and, depending on the circumstances, the person or result of something. By definition emotions *are a natural instinctive state of mind deriving from one's circumstances, mood or relationships with others.* It is an affective state of consciousness in which joy, sorrow, fear, hate, or the like, is experienced, as distinguished from cognitive and volitional states of consciousness, any of the feelings of joy, sorry, fear, hate, love, etc. (dictionary.com)

You do not want your emotions to control your marriage. That is a train wreck waiting to happen. If you have been guilty of this in the past (any time before reading this book) don't allow that emotion to cause you to feel self-pity or ashamed but instead consciously decide that after today, your emotions will no longer dictate your actions and behavior in your marriage and get to work.

Mastering Your Emotions (Respond vs. React) Reflection:

You just don't know how liberated I feel that I no longer allow my emotions to have its way. For me, Luke 9:23 couldn't be further from the truth in saying *"And he said to them all, if any man will come after me, let him deny himself, and take up his cross daily, and follow me."* Part of doing this process is to no longer allow your emotions to have the final say in your life or marriage. If you were to be honest with yourself; you will admit that, although emotionally, you may have felt better at the time; it did not contribute to the health of your marriage when you were unable to master your emotions. Trust me, I know, and that is why I want to help you on this journey. The 10 Week Wives Who Win Coaching Program was created for this very purpose, and it will be the ideal program to help you master your emotions and gain control back of your life and start Winning in your Marriage God's Way. Email us at officialwiveswhowin@gmail.com to sign up and learn more.

Chapter 14
Renew Your Mind, Transform Your Marriage (The Ultimate Makeover)

You have more power than you give yourself credit for in experiencing transformation in your marriage. You don't have to sit at the mercy seat and wait for your husband to change before you make a move. Do you recall me talking about the high road earlier? Well here is one of those instances whereas you being proactive and strategic in your approach will be beneficial to your marriage long term. Peter was not lying when he said that your husbands would not be won over by what you say, but by your character and conduct toward him (1 Peter 3:1). I know many wives are unable to change their character and conduct toward their husbands because of how they think about them for one reason or another. I don't know the details of your personal situation, but the fact that you made it to Chapter 14 tells me you are still very interested in WINNING in your marriage and most, if not all, of what you read thus far has helped you. Okay, if that is true; you are in an excellent position to evoke transformation in your marriage but guess what? It is going to start in your mind. Yes, the mind which is a part of your soul. If you didn't know; you are a triune being made up of mind, body and will and each of these play on the other. Let me break it down for you:

1. **Mind (Centralized Station)**

You have to get your mind right: Philippians 2:5, *Let this mind be in you which was also in Christ Jesus;* Romans 12:2, *Do not conform to the pattern of this world, but be transformed by the renewing of your mind. Then you will be able to test and approve what God's will is--his good, pleasing and perfect will.* It is a necessary Process to Win in your Marriage God's Way!! Once your mind gets right; your heart will follow. As a man thinketh; so is he or so he will become (Proverbs 23:7)

2. **Emotions aka the Heart (Receives and dissects the information received from the centralized station on how to act/be – who you are?)**

Emotions are energy in motion — they are up, down and all around. They are not the most reliable decision-making source. Your emotions receive information from your mind on how to process what your mind is thinking. You cannot have a heart full of hate, lies, and deceit if you want to build a healthy marriage. You cannot have animosity in your heart toward your husband and intimacy with God – the two cannot co-exist. You have to practice real love; the God kind of love and distribute that appropriately. Godly love is Agape love as mentioned in Chapter 9.

My dear children, let's not just talk about love; let's practice real love. This is the only way we'll know we're living truly, living in God's reality. It's also the way to shut down debilitating self-criticism, even when there is something to it. For God is greater than our worried hearts and knows more about us than we do ourselves. (1 John 3:18-20)

3. Will (Social) (Carry's out the information that was transmitted)

Once you have experienced a mind and emotional shift, then your will has no choice but to follow suit. It will carry out the ultimate plan or instructions. In almost all cases; this means changing what you spend the most time doing that is not contributing to the health and wealth of your marriage but in fact contributing to the destruction of your marriage.

Do you see how that works? So now it is up to you to change your mind about your husband and your marriage. Every negative, disheartening or bad thing you have ever thought about your husband regardless of what, get rid of it. Your ability to do this will not be self-motivated or encouraged, but it will take the help of others and, more importantly, God. The thing you seek the most in your husband is what you will continue to see in your husband. If you seek the bad and worst in him, that is what will continue to show up, but if you seek the good and best, that is what will begin to show up. You have to decide that if your husband is truly a good person and if he does love you then there is something there worth you finishing this book. You chose him, so I would hope that there is something there that caused you to not only accepts his offer in marriage, but that still has you there. This is one of the rare cases where I will tell you not to have a made up mind, and this is particularly toward your husband and marriage. There is no perfect marriage because there are no perfect people. Besides, WINNING in your marriage has nothing to do with perfection but all to do with purpose and intentions.

God created marriage between a man and woman to glorify him, so, in essence, marriage is less about you as husband and wife and more about Christ; His love and commitment demonstrated toward the church. One of the most controversial marriages in the Bible is that of Gomer and Hosea. God instructed Hosea to marry a prostitute, Gomer, in which he obliged. After being married for a while and having children; Gomer returned to her life as a prostitute while still married; had outside children and made up in her mind that she was going to do what she wanted. Clearly, Gomer had some deeply rooted and unresolved issues which God knew, and now her husband was finding out, and instead of him leaving her out there to continue to whore around; he listened to God and went and got his wife. In fact, he had to pay to get her back because she had reclaimed her life as a prostitute. Hosea expressed his hurt and disappointment to God, and I am sure he had some friends he turned to as well to get some things off of his chest. After all, the town where they lived; people knew what was going on, so he couldn't hide it. How embarrassing! While I am sure that Hosea wanted to go against God's command and divorce Gomer; he had the mind of Christ and as much as his flesh wanted to give up, throw in the towel and get rid of his wife; he chose to listen to God. God didn't and couldn't make him go get his wife; he had to choose. In the same way; I can't make you work on winning in your marriage by renewing your mind — it has to be a choice. I encourage you to read the book of Hosea, Chapters 1-3 in particular. I know this was a drastic example, but I wanted to use it because I firmly believe that no marriage is irreparable, however, I also know that it will take work to repair it and part of that work is renewing your mind.

Jesus dying on the cross for us is no different. He even asked God three times to change his mind and take the charge of dying for our sins away from him, but God refused. It was necessary. There had to be some extreme demonstrations of unconditional love for us to follow, not just for marriage sake, but for life as a whole. The clients I have worked with, and couples both my husband and I have spoken to, are not dealing with anything close to what Hosea or Jesus was faced with. In many cases, the love and or respect has been lost for other reasons, but these couples/clients do not want to walk away from their marriage; instead many of them are working toward rebuilding a solid foundation, and that started with them renewing their mind.

Renew Your Mind, Transform Your Life Reflection:

You made it! Thank you for sticking with me and being intentional about your next step in your marriage. We often hear that marriage is hard, but I beg to differ. Some of the decisions that we have to make are hard decisions because our flesh wants to be in control. I believe that is why marriage is the greatest examples of Christ love toward the church aka his bride. Marriage will bring out the good, the bad and the ugly truth of who you are and, let's face it — we can all use a dose of transformation in one area of another. Please don't think for a moment you can do this on your own. Don't set your marriage up for failure by taking this book, putting it to the side and coming up with your own way. In order for this to work; you have to be intentional about its success. I had countless people I had to connect with or depend on to some degree or another. God created us that way — relationally, in showing us that no one, not even Jesus, can do anything great alone. If you are not a part of the Wives Who Win community on Facebook; make that your goal, once you complete this book. You can find the community by going to **facebook.com/wiveswhowin.**

So, as we get ready to depart; I want to make sure you are ready to contribute to the success of your marriage and you have the necessary tools to do so. If you have no clue what to do next; I have a great resource that will help you. I created a 90 Day devotional entitled: A Winning Wife is a Praying Wife. It is a tool that will help you finish what you started when you decided to read this book in being a Wife Who Wins in her marriage every day. Are you ready? Email officialwiveswhowin@gmail.com to place your order. In the meantime, read the stories of some women that are WINNING in their marriage. It is my hope that these true and authentic stories will be a breath of fresh air to know that it is possible to Win in your Marriage God's Way

PART V

Chapter 15
Winning Wives Corner (Testimonials of Winning Wives)

For the remainder of this book; I will share some testimonials from ladies who are winning in their marriage. These women have been married for some years and while some caught onto winning early on in their marriage, it took others a while. Nonetheless, I want wives to know that you can make a decision to WIN in your marriage from Day one and work daily toward that goal.

Meet Winning Wife: Naomi A. Burrell
Age: 34
# of yrs. married: 10 years
City/state or country: Cockeysville, Maryland
Children? Yes
Blended Family? Yes

I met Naomi Rudisill-Burrell at our Brunch and Branding event in Maryland in 2016. From the moment I met her, we connected and we have been connecting ever since. She is an amazing person and what I most appreciate about her is her boldness, authenticity, and ability to take charge. She is known as Miss Be-Inspired and is the CEO of Be Inspired, LLC.

Here are a few nuggets Naomi shares about Winning in her Marriage:

Talk, talk, talk, talk, talk! That is one of the major keys to a healthy relationship! That is one of the things that have helped my husband and I pull through some of the hardest stuff! We talked it through TOGETHER! And most of all, we LISTENED! Don't be so eager to tell your truth that you don't open yourself to hear your husband's truth! If your husband is willing to share with you, don't shut him out! I am all ears now, and I learned that the hard way!

Another huge piece that has kept me and my husband going strong is that we find time to have fun together and often! It keeps us youthful, vibrant and attracted to each other! When we are doing the fun stuff together, we are giving ourselves permission for a moment to not worry about what is not going right or what we have to do, or pay or take care of! For a moment, we get to just be free and enjoy each other! That has worked for us! Our relationship is still growing and evolving, and I'm happy about that! #10yearsandcounting

Meet Winning Wife: Karen Guikoume
Age:34
# of yrs. married: 2
City/state or country: London
Children? Yes, 1 daughter
Blended family? Yes I had the opportunity to meet this Queen via Skype and absolutely love her spirit. Her

testimonial is so powerful and I know many will be blessed by it.

Here are a few nuggets Karen shares about Winning in her Marriage:

My moto
Your marriage, your ministry.
Change first
Be submissive

The first year of my marriage was a nightmare, the devil knocked me down.

I was desperate and angry at my husband.

He was not praying and was doing ungodly things.

I was thinking what did I get myself into, I wanted to divorce.

My husband left our home. It was a relief; I thought maybe God was separating us. God answered my prayer.

While my husband was away, I've realized two things; first, I was not obedient to my husband. My mom taught me that no man should walk over you and if your husband talk then talks back.

Second, I was trying to fix my husband with my flesh. I took God's place.

I've reconnected deeply with God. Now I know that God separated us for a good reason. He had a plan.☺

God remembered me. There is a scripture that says "we don't fight against flesh and blood"

I apologized to God for being disobedient and asked him to change me.

I stopped asking God change my husband; after all I was the one who claimed to be in Christ in this house.

I started to wake up at midnight and pray for my husband. I've asked God to heal me, put love in my heart for my husband and forgiveness in my heart for my husband.

My husband came back 8 months later, the obedient part was hard, but one thing that we have to know, satan is an accuser and he knows the bible, if you are not an obedient wife, your prayer won't even leave the Earth. They will be hindered.

I've started apologizing even when my husband was wrong and trying to bridle my tongue.

My midnight prayer was still going on, the first change that I've noticed was when I was talking about the gospel, and my husband listened to me.

Before then, he questioned me and thought I was trying to be super spiritual.

Today my husband is reading the Bible and listens to my advice. I know my husband will serve God. God has a plan for his life and I'm part of this plan.

My husband is not only my husband; he is member of body of Christ. God is waiting for him. This battle is not my battle it's the Lord.

Meet Winning Wife: Curtisha Grant
Age: 41
# of yrs. married: 20
City/state or country: Arlington, TX
Children? Yes, 2
Blended family? No

I met Tisha during my time in San Diego. She is so full of wisdom and undoubtedly loves God and family.

Here are a few nuggets Curtisha shares about Winning in her Marriage:

Titus 2: 3-6 Older women likewise are to exhibit behavior fitting for those who are holy, not slandering, not slaves to excessive drinking, but teaching what is good. 4 In this way they will train the younger women to love their husbands, to love their children, 5 to be self-controlled, pure, fulfilling their duties at home, kind, being subject to their own husbands, so that the message of God may not be discredited. I attached Titus because older women is not age in this content but it's maturity. Mature wives have a responsibility to model the word of God so that family principles are not discredited and his glory can be revealed in the home which ultimately strengthens the community. Keeping our families hydrated with love is exemplified through our self-control, kindness, submission and service. It requires a constant filling in order to continue pouring out. Wives must draw from the well of worship and the word in order to hydrate their families. Husbands need to see Gods perfect strength in operation through their wives. They need to witness Christ power resting on us. Not from a place of superiority, but from a place of assurance knowing that the fragrance of the home is saturated in worship and was ushered in through his favor (his wife) which validates the sufficiency of God's grace on the home. This has been the key to my marital strength, allowing the word of God to demonstrate the character of God through my actions. Then exercising the Divine strategy he gives me to produce more fruit in my home and marriage. Our commitment to each other brings strength to our marriage. Working together, succeeding together and even missing the mark at times together, become layers of strength to build on. We value our commitment to each other, respect the differences in each other but embrace and honor the sanctity of marriage. Who can God trust with his church? That's the reference he used when speaking of marriage. Who's willing to risk never fully understanding the mysteries of marriage but submitting you to the process? His strength is my strength and mine is his. The wisdom is leveraging your differences while building oneness. Keep your marriage hydrated!

Meet Winning Wife: Felicia Stevenson
Age: 46
# of yrs. married: 28 years
City/state or Country: Lanham, MD
Children? Yes - 4 children. 2 girls and 2 boys
Blended family? Yes

I have known <u>Felicia Stevenson</u> for 20+ yrs.... a very long time. She has played a tremendous role in my life and purpose. Felicia has been the most genuine example of a wife, mother, friend, leader, mentor, etc. She has touched the lives of women all across the world and continues to blaze the trail. I am so honored and blessed to know her.

Here are a few nuggets Felicia shares about Winning in Marriage:

When we begin to love our spouse like we love Christ, marriage will become so much easier! I have been with my husband for 28 years. February 13, 2017, we celebrated 25 years of marriage! Problems? Yes! Disagreements? Yes! Arguments and feelings of wanting to give up on my marriage? Absolutely! It wasn't until we began to put God 1st in our marriage that we began to build a stronger marriage the way God has ordained it to be. 28 years.....nothing that my husband did, nothing that I did......it was all because of God! Along with keeping God first, Communication, Respect, and Trust are the best recipes for a successful marriage. More importantly, keep others out of your marriage and that includes family! The union is between the husband and wife; you two have become one and whatever you go through, go through it together. Good times, bad times, the ups and the downs, do it together! Lastly, never stop dating your mate! I don't care how busy things get; I don't care how low funds are.....once a week, date your mate! It can be an in-house date, out house date, or walk in the park date, no excuse! Commit to one day a week and stick to it. I can't express how important this is.

Meet Winning Wife: Ne'Shama Bonneau
Age: 27
# of yrs. married: 7 years
Country: England, UK
Children: Yes
Blended family: No

I ran into Ne'Shama at an event my niece was hosting stateside for young girls/women who desired to restore their love back to Christ. When I met her, I can remember saying to myself how cute she was. I did not know at the time that she was married with two precious small children and that she was a military wife. As I got to know her more; I discovered that she is such a jewel. She desired transformation, and she sought after it. Any and everything to do with transformation that was offered through our parent company, Detour Movement Inc.; she bought into it, both literally and figuratively. I liked that about her. In fact, I loved that about her - the fact that she hungered and thirst, not only after knowledge, but after change, said to me that she had what it took to be a Wife Who Wins.

Here are a few nuggets Ne'Shama shares about Winning in Marriage:

When the world is so loud, it gets tough to be centered in your relationship with God, but I urge you not to take this for granted. In the beginning, I lead my life, marriage, and home through my flesh. I knew God, but He was not the head of my life and center of my marriage and family. As I began to understand that my marriage was my FIRST ministry, my mind shifted. To be a wife who wins in her marriage, you must keep God number one. By allowing Him a place to dwell within, gives you access to a level of prosperity and love that is unlike anything you could ever fathom. Trust your marriage to Him. When I did that, things begin to turn completely around. God will supply the courage you need to keep your marriage strong in the midst of chaos, because, I promise you, every day is not sunshine and rainbows. If I can leave you anything; I will leave this: Strive to delve deeper into becoming a better spirit driven helpmate for your husband. Self-development and growth is a necessity for a healthy marriage. Also, remember that the vows you took were just the beginning and it is going to take intentional daily acts to continue to achieve the marriage that God has for you.

Meet Winning Wife: Shauntay Dunning
Age: 31
# of yrs. married: 4 years 3 months
Country: Dorchester, SC
Children: Yes
Blended family: Yes

I met Shauntay December 2015 at an event we were hosting: Charleston Brunch and Branding event. She was one of the first to go through our Kingdom Builder 365 program, designed for current and inspiring entrepreneurs or ministry leaders who need more clarity for their business or ministry and help in identifying and attracting their ideal client. I have watched her grow leaps and bounds in her personal life, marriage, and business. Her life is a true testament of what transformation looks like, and I know that it would not have been possible without her continued pursuit, persistence and passion to experience success in every area of her life.

Here are a few nuggets Shauntay shares about Winning in Marriage:

Wives Who Win have had a huge impact on my marriage as well as my life. It has truly been a blessing to work with these phenomenal women: Jill and Treal. Through this movement of *"Wives Who Win"* I have learned to be more open in communication with my husband and how to show more affection. I have learned how to let go of *"pride"* and *"independence."* When God equally yoke two individuals together, understand that you are now one.

The best part was truly letting go of my fears and insecurity by fully trusting my husband. We must get over our past hurt, so it will not hinder our future. I am now able to cope with our son's mom and work together in unity on behalf of our son. Always remember that it is not always about us and how we feel. Sometimes we have to take ourselves out of the equation and focus on others for a greater outcome or impact. Rules to a great marriage: Keep God first, never lose the love you had at first sight, Spend quality time with your husband and children and the most important of them all, Remember to spend time with yourself: Relax, Treat Yourself and Rest!!!

Simple Tips to Winning for Wives and Wives to be:

Encouragement for wives and wives to be! I want to dispel some lies you may have been told or even witnessed in marriages around you throughout your lifetime. Unfortunately, the norm of marriage for you may have included you being told over and over that all marriages go through trials and tribulations (extreme hell on earth) and that these things are necessary to have a great marriage. I do believe that marriages will be faced with adversity and opposition, after all, one of the greatest examples of Christ unconditional love for the church (his bride) and God's unconditional love toward us is the marriage covenant.

However, I disagree with the fact that you have to constantly go through hell in order to have a great marriage. I also disagree with the fact that you have to be married for almost a lifetime in order to experience the joys of marriage. While marriage does bring out the good, bad and ugly (your true and bold self); it doesn't have to be painful or pitiful. I came up with four reasons why so many marriages stay in *stuck mode* and on the endless crazy cycle.

1. **Refusal to grow up.** You deny or discard the fact that personal growth and development will contribute to Winning in your Marriage God's Way.

2. **Accountability to No one.** You attempt to do life on your own, and when you get married, you have the same mindset. Not only are couples not accountable to each other, but, in most cases, they aren't accountable to themselves or God.

3. **Take God out of the equation** and only seek Him when things are too much for you to bear. God created marriage between a man and woman so who better to give instructions on how it should work then Him. He is the CEO of the marriage convenant and I can guarantee you if you follow His lead; your marriage will have a 100% success rate. All too often, God is removed from the equation, and couples try to work things out in their own strength and intellect. You will exhaust and completely overwhelm yourself trying to figure it out and your well will run dry. None of us are smart or strategic enough to do this thing alone. Marriage is a God thing - Point Blank Period. If God is/was the missing link; give Him a front seat to your marriage table and keep him there.

4. **Selfishness/Self-Seeking.** 1 Corinthians 13:5 says "Love does not dishonor others, **it is not self-seeking**, it is not easily angered, and it keeps no record of wrongs." I have told individuals on countless occasions that if you are selfish, you will fail at life, in your marriage and as a parent.

Marriage isn't about you — it is about God and His love for you. Marriage was created to glorify God, and, in doing so; your flesh must take a backseat. The sacrifices, adjustments and compromising that will be necessary to win in your marriage God's way will not be possible if you are a selfish person. You might as well hang that up. On a daily basis, you have to consider the other person (you chose to spend the rest of your life with) when you are making decisions, even if you feel like what you are doing does not or will not affect them. The whole basis behind this is including the other person in your life as a whole and not leaving any stones unturned or ambiguity to muster at any given time. Yes, I know when you were single you could do what you wanted, when you wanted to, and how you wanted to do it, but now that you are married; that selfish mind and attitude has to go. If you want your marriage to be a WIN WIN, start looking at opportunities that will benefit us, not just you.

Winning daily in your marriage will require you getting rid of the R.A.T.S. (Refusal to Grow | Accountability to No one | Take God out of the Equation | Selfishness/Self-Seeking). It is time to call pest control and deal with the root of stagnant or failing marriages. It is my goal that every word written in this book will prepare and positions you to be a Wife Who Wins regardless of your current marital status:

In order to WIN in your marriage, you do NOT have to:

- Be married for a long time before you can experience true happiness.

- Experience all sorts of extreme hell on earth to build a healthy marriage.
- Give your husband ultimatums.
- Go around singing the "marriage is hard" blues - that only puts ammunition in the air for Satan's use.
- Walk around dragging your feet because you have been told time and time again that *"marriage is so much work"* so now you feel more like a slave, than a contributing partner aka wife.
- Try and change your husband by using manipulation and deceit.
- Focus on what your husband is doing wrong and pick apart his life.
- Constantly point out your husband's flaws and insecurities so you feel better.
- Shut down and pout, in hopes of getting your way.
- Read your husband's mind or desire for him to read yours.

But you DO have to:

- Make a daily decision to WIN in your marriage and create happiness.
- Deal with conflict when it arises from a healthy manner and learn from it, so that growth takes place.
- Be on the same page with your husband at all times, even when you don't agree with him.
- Make the hard decisions by denying your flesh every single day – Luke 9:23.

- Invest your time and resources in your marriage by doing things such as reading a book, listening to audios, cd's, attending a live event (i.e. conference, workshop, seminar etc.) or participating in a mentoring or coaching program that will help you be a better wife, so you can create a better life.

- Be the change you desire to see, and you will see what you want to see. What you sow in your marriage is what will grow.

- Focus on what your husband is doing right and continue to build him up in word and deed.

- Always take a look at your own life; focus on being a better you and God will do the rest.

- Keep the lines of communication open and often ask God to bridle your tongue and soften your husband's heart so your words are graceful, life-giving and well received.

- Share your concerns, likes, dislikes with your husband and be open to hearing his and be ready to make adjustments within reason and as needed.

Stay Connected so you can Maintain your Winning Status!

Facebook *Fan Page*: facebook.com/wiveswhowin

Facebook   *Group:*
https://www.facebook.com/groups/273276863146874/

Periscope: https://www.periscope.tv/wiveswhowin

Website: www.wiveswhowin.com

Weekly Prayer: Every Wednesday @ 5:30AM EST: 712-451-1083; access code: 457207#

Email: officialwiveswhowin@gmail.com

Bibliography

The Odds are Against Us By Kimberly Sayer-Giles, April 2011 https://www.ksl.com/?sid=15303576).Stepfamilies:

What Is the Function of the Earth's Core? By Emma Woodhouse, 2017 http://sciencing.com/function-earths-core-8782098.html

About the Author

Treal aka the Wife Coach is a Life & Marriage Transformational Strategist, National Speaker and Author. She is also the Co-Founder of Detour Movement Inc (DMI) and Visionary behind the Wives Who Win (WWW) Movement which combined reaches over 10,000 married and single women globally. Treal is one of the leading contributors of a private online community (DMI Kingdom Women Lounge) that consist of 1.6k women. Treal is the co-host of the annual "SHE'S F.I.R.E" Love & Relationship Conference that gathers 100+ women from all across the world to come together for two impactful days of Life, Relationship and Business Transformation. Treal is extremely passionate about positioning Wives to Win in their Marriage against ALL odds and have made a personal commitment to help 1,000,000 wives to reach and maintain a Winning status in their marriage.

A Wife Who Wins is more than just a fancy title. In fact, a Wife Who Wins is a wife who is a Warrior in the spirit. She is spiritually grounded. She has a proven relationship with God, and it is evident to those around her. She is an Influencer, Integrity minded and Intentional about everything that she does. This woman is trustworthy, honest and speaks the truth always. Every decision she makes for her marriage is Intentional and contributes to the wealth and health of her marriage. She uses her Influence for good and not evil toward her husband and others. Lastly, a wife who wins makes a decision to Non-negotiable decision to Never give up on her marriage. Despite the odds, she has made a declaration that divorce is not an option. This book is intended to encourage wives and wives-to-be all over the world that they too can choose to win in their marriage. Daily, you have to decide to Forgive, choose to Love, decide to Accept one another for which they are, choose to display Grace and decide to submit one to another. Marriage is an investment, and what you put in, you will get in return. The seeds you sow today, will determine the harvest you reap tomorrow!

Made in the USA
Columbia, SC
31 July 2017